The failing qu~~an~~g~~e~~ ~~-~~

The failing quango state

Dr Richard Norrie

CIVITAS

First published
April 2023

© Civitas 2023

55 Tufton Street
London SW1P 3QL

Email: books@civitas.org.uk

ISBN: 978-1-912581-44-3

Printed by 4edge Limited, Essex

Independence: Civitas: Institute for the Study of Civil
Society is a registered educational charity (No. 1085494)
and a company limited by guarantee (No. 04023541).
Civitas is financed from a variety of private sources to
avoid over-reliance on any single or small group of donors.

All the Institute's publications seek to further its objective
of promoting the advancement of learning. The views
expressed are those of the authors, not of the Institute.

Contents

Author

Dr Richard Norrie joined Civitas in 2020 and is Director of the Statistics and Policy Research Programme.

Introduction

We are in a time of great uncertainty as we experience and try to make sense of the consequences of the lockdown in response to the Covid-19 pandemic. Inflation is back, with many families wondering how on earth they will pay their bills. Vladimir Putin's senseless and cruel invasion of Ukraine has brought war back to the European continent, and where it will lead is hard to say but remains a fear for all concerned. Our departure from the European Union has led to much finger-pointing from all sides. Supporters point to deluded and aloof politicians who lost touch with the values of ordinary people. Recalcitrant opponents, in turn, single out politicians as reckless with the nation's future and pursuing pure pie in the sky. The country has lost its lodestone in the death of Her Majesty Queen Elizabeth II. The National Health Service is overwhelmed, something lockdowns were supposed to prevent, while we have an open border that seems so hard to close, despite the Brexit promise of 'taking back control'. To cap it all off, we had the ignominious 49 days of Liz Truss' premiership coming after 10 weeks of the Conservative Party choosing her.

Yet for all the uncertainty, fury and recriminations, we lose sight of the fact that we are not just governed by politicians. £223.9 billion was spent by so-called arm's length bodies (ALBs) in 2020, which employed 318,714 people. As a percentage of total government expenditure, that is 21 per cent.[1] These are defined by their independence from ministers – and a strong degree of distance from electoral power. Such numbers pertain to just a subset of the country's vast array of 'quangos', an acronym standing for 'quasi autonomous non-governmental organisations'. While this term has common currency, it is a misnomer in that these are very much part of governmental functions with the power to set rules, adjudicate, and impose services.

This report reveals them to be both nominally accountable to parliament yet somehow escaping serious repercussions for shoddy service. The government does not have a good grasp on them, with no certainty as to how many even exist. The Cabinet Office keeps an official list, only some organisations are allowed to exist off-record. The Coalition Government promised a 'bonfire of the quangos,' which to some extent did happen, only it is hard to know if this was achieved by reclassification or not. At the same time, through a series of case studies looking at prominent quangos presented in this report, we see a pattern of failing at their bread-and-butter tasks, sometimes spectacularly, while embracing ostentatious political objectives such as radical gender and racial equality agendas, as well as the new hair-shirt idealism of 'net-zero'. But if they are bad at the basics, how will they ever achieve the ambitious? Moreover, such goals are ill-defined or not even defined, meaning there comes a point where all this just proves insulting to the citizenry.

Obviously, this is a state of affairs that cannot be allowed to persist, despite those who would happily do so right up until it is too late. The Queen's funeral showed how we can get things right, producing a ceremony involving thousands that achieved flawless synchronisation as well as solemn grace and poignancy. It was a masterpiece fit for the master constitutional monarch. But once over, we are still confronted with the same old sludge of often self-serving governance, at arm's length or otherwise.

We have (another) new prime minister and government tasked with sorting it all out. It is a considerable task, with this report finding numerous examples of quangos malfunctioning, often to disastrous effect. The Bank of England fails to predict and reign in inflation. The British Business Bank inadvertently doles out money to Eastern European criminals. The Water Services Regulation Authority (OFWAT) fails to crack down on massive amounts of water leakage and sewage dumping in our rivers. It takes months to get a driver's licence. The Scientific Advisory Group for Emergencies (SAGE) puts us all under house arrest based on wild predictions, akin to digital soothsaying. Meanwhile, unelected officials earn huge sums of money with little scrutiny, leading to the question, why would anyone stand for elected office if things are so good for the unelected?

The government needs to take back control of *itself*, with democratically elected politicians in power as much as possible, if only on a point of principle. Certainly, the technocratic argument has been refuted by recent evidence. Technocrats are no better placed, nor fleeter of foot, and are weighed down by their own sets of incentives, often perverse. What remains is to convince politicians that they actually want both power over these things as well as responsibility. The argument will go, that if you really want to achieve things in politics, to make a success of Brexit, then you will need power over the institutions above and beyond the vested interests that coalesce within them.

Gratitude is extended to Jim McConalogue and Frank Young of Civitas for their suggestions and input, as well as the helpful comments of anonymous reviewers.

1

Theory

Introduction

This chapter begins with defining what is meant by 'quangos', by going through what official classifications there are. It is argued that through all the vagueness encountered, the government does not have much by way of control or oversight, with the Cabinet Office found wanting. It is further argued that there is considerable political resistance to attempts by the government to regain control, most notable in clashes over public appointments.

What are quangos?

The term 'quango' is an acronym which stands for 'quasi-autonomous non-governmental organisation'. It is a misnomer in that these are often very much governmental, being branches of the state, funded largely by taxation and which may set regulations and take decisions. Nevertheless, it is one with popular currency and perhaps more widely understood than those used in the government's own nomenclature, for which it should be understood as an umbrella term.

Perhaps the closest direct synonym would be 'public bodies,' which if defined are done so more in reference to their function and justification, at least according to a Cabinet Office document. They are bodies 'carrying out public functions' with a 'greater degree of independence' from government ministers. They provide 'independent advice and expertise on technical, scientific or other complex issues', 'independent regulation', 'investigation', 'adjudication', 'ombudsman services', 'appeals', 'funding', and 'commercial and health services'.[2] In addition, many of the major museums and art galleries join the list. Another term used is 'arm's length bodies,' (ALBs) although there appears to be some disagreement in what this applies to, when contrasting the Cabinet Office's usage with that of, say, the view of the think-tank the Institute for Government.

A subset of public bodies are 'non-departmental public bodies' (NDPBs), defined as a having a 'role in the processes of national government, but is not a government department, or part of one, and which accordingly operates to a greater or lesser extent at arm's length from ministers.'[3] An imbalanced equation exists whereby 'day-to-day decisions' are independent of ministers and civil servants, yet ministers are 'ultimately responsible to parliament' for its independence, effectiveness and efficiency. Ministers are further accountable to parliament for their expenditure.

Official arguments for such bodies are self-serving and commit the logical fallacy of *begging the question*, meaning to assume the premise for something you wish to justify rationally. For example, the Cabinet Office document states a NDPB will be appropriate, if 'the function needs to be carried out at arm's length from ministers e.g. regulation functions, decisions on funding.' But who decides on the definition of need and by what threshold is this met? Another example is 'when expert advice is required by ministers on technical/ specialised issues'. But is that not what civil servants are for, and can government not solicit a range of opinions from civil society? Such reasoning assumes governance needs freedom from elected officials, but this flies in the face of basic democratic principles.

NDPBs further subdivide into:

1. Executive NDPBs – set up by ministers to 'carry out administrative, commercial, executive or regulatory functions on behalf of the government'.

2. Advisory NDPBs – established on ministerial authority to provide 'independent expert advice or to provide input into the policy-making process'.

3. Tribunal NDPBs – have 'jurisdiction in a specialised field of law', and operate 'under statutory provisions and decide the rights and obligations of private citizens towards a government department or public authority.'[4]

Other types of public bodies include public corporations, public broadcasting authorities, central banks, nationalised industries, and NHS bodies. You also have non-ministerial departments and executive agencies. The former are governmental departments 'in their own right' but without their own ministers.[5] The latter 'allow the delivery of executive functions of government' carried out 'separately from – but within a policy and resources framework set by – a primarily policy focused department'. These may deliver services, carry out statutory or regulatory functions, or carry out 'functions separate to the core role of the sponsor department'.[6]

Evidently, the distinctions between these different types of government institution are, to a large degree, artificial. What they all have in common is minimal ministerial direction. There is an argument for this, where a public body is acting as an independent regulator. But closer inspection will reveal we are often talking about technocrats, with conflicts of interest which clash with the principle of independence. Their activities are usually opaque and not well understood by the electorate. Why should these people enjoy less scrutiny and accountability while the democratically elected politicians have to suffer for their maladministration in parliament and at elections?

Regulation and accountability

According to the Cabinet Office, ALBs are overseen by their sponsoring departments. Their accounting officers and government ministers are accountable 'directly to parliament' for 'overall effectiveness' of ALBs. Cabinet Office ministers are further responsible for approving the creation of new ones. A 'sponsor' is appointed to manage the relationship between the arm's length body and its government department, who put in place 'clear accountability arrangements'.[7] It is important not to understate the minister's responsibility and power over ALBs – they set the direction of policy and can hire and fire their chief executive, according to official rules. However, such rules, or at least the relationships between ALBs, ministers and sponsoring departments, not to mention the rest of governmental apparatuses (for example, human resources) inevitably reach towards vagueness. It is possible to imagine they can provide enough leeway for much to go on without the hard-pressed minister having the slightest idea.[8]

Cabinet Office data exist on some measures of quango accountability, although just for a subset of those classified as ALBs. Those absent from its official list operate to a lower level of accountability, or at least do not appear to be accountable. According to analysis by the Institute for Government (IFG), around 90 per cent of ALBs have a published register of interests. Roughly 75 per cent are regulated by the Office of the Commission of Public

Appointments (OCPA), 51 per cent have been reviewed in the last five years, half publish minutes of their meetings, while around 15 per cent hold public meetings. These figures would leave substantially low levels of oversight for many public bodies.[9]

The same IFG analysis claims a recent drop in accountability, but that is perhaps overstating things. While most indicators have budged very little since 2016, there is one substantial drop – and that is in the number being reviewed in the last five years. This fell 15 percentage points since 2016. The number holding public meetings also dropped somewhat over the same period.[10]

Salaries

Running a quango can be highly lucrative, sometimes eye-wateringly so. Some bosses work just a few days a week or year, making it difficult to produce a ranking of who gets paid the most or to account for the bill in full. Day rates can reach as much as £600. In the case of Lord Deben (John Gummer), his day rate is £1,000, for his work on the Climate Change Committee, covering 36 days per year.[11] Accounting officers can also be well-rewarded, with many reaching into the hundreds of thousands. Table 1.1 sets out some examples of both.[12] For comparison, the salary of the prime minister is around £157,000, and for a cabinet minister, £150,000 (inclusive of salaries as MPs).[13]

Judging from the figures, it is hard to imagine why anyone would want to seek elected office when you can command considerable power within a quango for much more money, but with far less of the grief that comes with politics. Moreover, this unelected bureaucracy of officials is often where true power lies, so it is a far better choice for talented individuals with a public service ethic who want to 'make a difference'. Plus, they face lower levels of scrutiny and accountability thrown into the bargain. That contrasts sharply with what parliamentarians have to put up with.

Table 1.1. Salaries of selected quango officials in 2020

Name	Organisation	Role	Salary
Michael Lockwood	Independent Office for Police Conduct	Chair	£175,000 p.a.
Martin Cave	Ofgem	Chair	£160,000 - £165,000 p.a. (4 days per week)
Lisa Osofsky	Serious Fraud Office	Chair	£181,800 p.a.
Jonson Cox	OFWAT	Chair	£125,000 p.a. (3 days per week)
Elizabeth Denham	Information Commissioners Office	Chair	£160,000 p.a.
Allan Cook	High Speed 2 Ltd	Chair	£230,000 p.a. (3 days per week)
Sir Peter Roth	Competition Appeal Tribunal	Chair	£185,000 - £190,000 p.a. (171 days)
Sir Ciaran Devane	British Council	Accounting officer	£200,000 - £205,000 p.a.
Sir Simon Bollom	Defence Equipment and Support	Accounting officer	£280,000 p.a.
Simon Blanchflower	East West Rail Company	Accounting officer	£220,000 p.a.
Ian Cumming	Health Education England	Accounting officer	£205,000 - £210,000 p.a.
Mark Thurston	High Speed 2 Ltd	Accounting officer	£620,000 - £624,999 p.a.
Nick Walkley	Homes England	Accounting officer	£215,000 - £220,000 p.a.
Dame Lynne Owens	National Crime Agency	Accounting officer	£223,441 p.a.
Amanda Pritchard	NHS Improvement	Accounting officer	£255,000 - £260,000 p.a.
David Peattie	Nuclear Decommissioning Authority	Accounting officer	£498,921 p.a.

Source: Cabinet Office.

Criticism from parliament

The House of Commons Public Accounts Committee (PAC), chaired by Dame Meg Hillier, published a report on ALBs in September 2021, as a sequel to an earlier inquiry carried out by the same committee in 2016.[14] Government departments were criticised for their running of ALBs. The report offers a staunch rebuke to the Cabinet Office in particular for failing on its pledges to bring about greater scrutiny.

The Cabinet Office has 'policy responsibility for the governance and accountability' of ALBs, providing guidance and support as well as being jointly responsible with Her Majesty's Treasury (HMT) for approving new ones. Yet the PAC report concluded the Cabinet Office was pretty much out at sea, and that it needed to 'get a grip'.

The Committee states that 'in 2016 we called for the Cabinet Office to use its unique position at the centre of government to ensure that the departments improve the way they manage their business through arm's length bodies'. It notes that the Cabinet Office published a 'Code of Good Practice' that set out the 'principles of effective working'. However, the Cabinet Office did not monitor whether these were adhered to. PAC also noted the Cabinet Office promised in 2016 to review all ALBs by the end of 2020, but managed just one third.

Moreover, it is made clear by the Committee that the Cabinet Office has waved its own rules for establishing new ALBs. Not one of the 24 'business cases' or economic rationales for new ALBs approved between 2016 and 2020 met all the requirements set out by the Cabinet Office. One quarter failed to include a requisite 'costs/benefits' analysis, yet were approved anyway. And despite official guidelines that ALBs should be a 'last resort,' more than one third did not 'rigorously consider the alternatives' to setting up a new one. As the PAC report states, failing to do so 'can lead to substandard governance and performance'.

The Committee bemoans a 'lack of consistency' in how ALBs work with departments and how they are held to account. It notes that ALBs and departments have 'framework agreements' and 'accounting officer system statements' that formalise the operations between them. Yet four out of 10 'framework agreements' (documents that establish an ALB's remit) examined by the National Audit Office (NAO) were out of date, and three 'system statements' had not been updated since 2017.

For the Committee, it is up to the Cabinet Office to raise its game to enforce consistency and accountability. While there is something to be said for this argument, there are two problems, one to do with structure, the other incentives. PAC is expecting the Cabinet Office to improve relationships between other departments and ALBs, that are often ambiguous or varied. Sponsoring departments already have accountability for oversight of ALBs, so *where* the line lies between them and the Cabinet Office, with its own set of expectations, will be difficult to establish.

Secondly, the Cabinet Office is subject to the same perverse incentives as ALBs, in that they are both tax-payer funded and often large bureaucracies, whereby deadweight can be indulged at others' expense, lending itself towards lethargy, rent-seeking and mediocrity. Moreover, regulation in this case is often civil servants appraising other civil servants in ALBs that they might conceivably work in one day. Indeed, as the PAC report states, 'the Cabinet Office told us that the support it offers is guided by what departments and arm's length bodies want to see'. In other words, the tail might very well be wagging the dog. Under such circumstances, it is hard to see the Cabinet Office working wonders, and its sluggishness – as evidenced by the PAC – may stand as attestation to these arguments.

Diversity

Observers have noticed an obsession with all things diversity and inclusion within quangos, evidenced by the proliferation of jobs in this area. The PAC report might further be criticised for its stance on diversity in public appointments across ALBs. It notes the Cabinet Office 'does not have a plan in place to improve diversity across the appointments process' and calls on it to address this. Yet, it does not tell us how diverse public appointments are or how diverse they should be. In any case, analysis published by the Institute for Government shows in 2019/20, 51 per cent of appointees were women, against a benchmark of 48 per cent of the economically active population. Fifteen per cent were from ethnic minority groups, compared to 13 per cent of those economically active.[15] So not much of a problem against these benchmarks, while a reported shortfall for disabled people can easily be put down to competitive advantages between those able and those disabled.

In fact, the data show public appointments are actually *overly diverse* once you accept that there is no reason why any groups' share in a given walk of life should reflect its share of the population as a whole. Better benchmarks would include the share of ethnic minorities graduating from Russell Group universities at the turn of the century, since these would be the best placed candidates for positions of leadership some 20 years later – around nine to 10 per cent.[16] Or the shares of women who prioritise career over family, since getting to the top usually requires such sacrifices or choices, put at about one third.[17]

Against such benchmarks, we see possibly a prescription

for too much diversity across ALBs. The IFG data further show that ethnic diversity was at around 10 per cent and constant from 2002 to 2019, rising artificially thereafter, while for gender, it was at around 35 per cent and constant prior to 2014, before its rise. What this would imply is that people have been appointed, in part, on the basis of their sex or ethnicity, and this will entail some inappropriate appointees reaching positions of power and responsibility. These are problems not considered by the PAC.

The government's response to PAC

The government responded to PAC in December 2021, accepting both its conclusions and recommendations. Since the PAC report is a rebuke to the Cabinet Office, the government's actions that it commits itself to largely concern the Cabinet Office. The government will be asking it for a plan, only the actions themselves are spelled out in *Mandarinese*. They sound substantive but could mean everything, anything, or nothing to any skilled Sir Humphrey willing to listen. For example, the government will write to PAC to provide 'an update on our emerging work on a Public Bodies Strategy', and 'using departments' assessment of risks and their management across their ALBs to inform the public bodies programme of focused and coordinated reviews to examine the effectiveness of the management of areas of significant risk'. In any case, the response reads as a continuation of the status quo but with added resolve – must try harder![18]

The response is sufficiently bland as to be readily overlooked and forgotten. It is a masterpiece of evasion through complacency. However, it should be said the initial PAC inquiry viewed the issue of ALBs through a very narrow prism, as a technical issue to be resolved by technocratic tinkering. Questions of legitimacy, political capture and waste were generally not asked. Finally, the flaw with blaming the Cabinet Office is that you fail to ask whether individual departments themselves, that are supposedly the 'sponsors' of ALBs, are fulfilling their responsibilities, as well as the bodies in question.

Public appointments

The question of who heads public bodies that are supposed to be politically neutral will inevitably be political. Such is the nature of politics, and particularly when so many aspiring political actors have such little chance at the ballot box. Having a sympathetic head of a quango would be a great boon since they have much power, and so public appointments are considered rich prizes.

There have been recently some big rows over appointments to head up the Charity Commission, Ofcom, and the Office for Students, with actions of nepotism levelled at the government. According to the Institute for Government, 'the level of interest in appointments from No.10 has been much higher since Boris Johnson became prime minister'. It found the number of 'exceptional appointments' made without competition rose from around 20 in 2017 to more than 50 in 2021.[19]

In mitigation, it might be argued that this was in fact a necessary response from an elected pro-Brexit government, to break the predominantly pro-EU political establishment's stranglehold on the non-democratically-elected state. There was nothing wrong in principle with such appointments which were vetted in the usual manner, and persisting with the usual methods would have presented only the usual suspects for the usual appointments, it might be argued. This, the thinking goes, is simply the Tories putting their supporters into power in the same way that Labour did under Blair.

Nor does the report from the Institute for Government seem too concerned about the resistance from the quango sector to the will of the government it is supposed to serve. The recommendations it makes in a recent report include to 'remove ministers' ability to appoint a candidate judged unappointable by an assessment panel', and 'limit ministerial decision-making to the start and end of an appointment process', 'subject appointments to roles that scrutinise the actions of politicians to a veto from the relevant House of Commons select committee'.[20] Such measures will likely ensure bland appointments palatable only to the left-leaning, pro-state, pro-EU faction that has a vested interest in more governance while unable to coordinate the state's newfound independence.

According to a separate analysis from the Institute, the number of public appointees with political affiliations declined to six per cent in 2020/21. Moreover, its analysis shows the Johnson years saw an increase in the proportion of Conservative affiliates in public appointments. 2020/21 was one of the few years where there were more Tory than Labour appointees, although they were outnumbered, once you account for other political parties. Eight out of nine new chairs who declared themselves politically active were Conservative supporters. Contrast this picture with the height of the Blair years, when up to 20 per cent of all appointees were political partisans, mostly Labour. Such preferences continued in the Cameron and May years; although numbers reduced somewhat – in most years Labour supporters tended to outnumber Tories.[21]

Let us examine in detail some of the sagas surrounding public appointments:

i) **Paul Dacre**, the former editor of *The Daily Mail*, was the government's preferred choice to chair OFCOM, the communications regulator in 2020. He withdrew from the running after he was ruled 'unappointable' for the role by an interview panel, due reportedly to his 'style and appropriateness'.[22] Critics pointed to his past criticisms of the BBC as well as having reportedly been fined for not paying for a BBC licence.[23] In his own words, he described the experience of the selection process as,

'the civil service will control (and leak) everything; the process could take a year in which your life will be put on hold; and if you are possessed of an independent mind and are un-associated with the liberal/left, you will have more chance of winning the lottery than getting the job.'

He further added that he was ruled out because he had 'revealed strong convictions that were incompatible with the role of an independent chairmanship.'[24]

ii) **Lord James Wharton**, a Conservative Peer and former Tory MP, was appointed in 2021 to chair the Office for Students, which regulates higher education in England. Critics pointed to his political closeness to Boris Johnson, as well as his lack of experience in higher education and an apparent political bias in the selection panel.[25] This came after the journalist and free schools advocate Toby Young resigned (2018) from the board of the same organisation after past offensive and controversial statements came to light.[26]

iii) **Martin Thomas** was appointed to chair the Charity Commission in 2021, only to resign within days after his conduct while working at the charity Women for Women International UK was questioned. Yet, out of four complaints, only one was partially upheld and pertained to 'comments he had allegedly made to an employee on a Zoom call'. He has also had some sort of political relationship with Johnson in the past.[27] His replacement, Orlando Fraser, was appointed despite rejection from the parliamentary Digital, Culture, Media and Sport (DCMS) committee. Although it recognised Fraser's 'potential to do the job', it complained of an 'unimaginative approach to his recruitment' and a lack of diversity in the shortlisting. This is despite public appointments having perfectly defensible levels of ethnic and gender diversity, with levels in line with population shares, at least on the terms that the argument is usually made.[28] This came after Tina Stowell was appointed in 2018, despite being rejected by the same committee, citing concerns over her supposed lack of experience.[29]

All such figures will be palatable to some, objectionable to others. There does seem, however, to be a concerted effort to frustrate appointments made by the elected government, of people who are intended to disrupt the status quo. Such appointments are in theory, at least, to be welcomed given the sluggish performance of so many quangos that often fall into incompetence and hubris. It should also be pointed out that those who object the loudest are inevitably political partisans themselves who would rather somebody else, that they approve of, get the job. The recommendations made by many, including by the report from the Institute for Government, would only strengthen their hand.

So, what's the problem with quangos?

The move towards quangos gained impetus in the late 1980s, when a review of civil service reform by Sir Robin Ibbs (1988) recommended them as a model to circumvent the perceived monolithic elements of the civil service, with its preference for centrally set rules and risk aversion. However, it is arguable that such ills have only remanifested themselves within the quangos themselves, along with the scourge of 'group think'. Often the concerns of those who run them are far removed from those of the general public, with the starkest being views over Brexit, but also modish political concerns to do with race and gender equality.

There are two further theoretical problems that count against them. Firstly, democratic, in that expert advice or imposed regulations, which are inescapably political, get presented as unquestionable authoritative facts that bypass parliament where they can be properly scrutinised. The 'net zero' target based on the advice of the Climate Change Committee is one such example. As my Civitas colleague Jim McConalogue has written, quangos 'often enable enlarged [governmental] executives populated by governing elites to remove important, sometimes contested issues from wider public debate'.[30]

The second is a dilution of accountability, whereby quangos tend to face less public scrutiny than government ministers, and usually after things have gone wrong. Their empowerment also serves to impede the accountability of elected politicians in that the ministerial direction for a given policy and its implementation are divorced from one another. For example, you will see quangos such as the British Business Bank venturing into the realm of regional equality, although this is very much in line with the 'levelling up' agenda that takes its lead from on high.

There are also important constitutional implications, not just relevant to the political theorist but to us all. If quangos are permitted to come into existence, at the discretion of the Cabinet Office that is unwilling to enforce its own rules, then how is it not fair to say we are seeing the incremental encroachment of a new entrenched elite into spheres of governance that ought to be the preserve of free individuals, or more aptly, individuals we can be freely rid of come election time should we wish it? The political theorist Martin Loughlin has argued that elected ministers have been replaced by political innovations, either domestic or European, that operate beyond the reach of democratic accountability. This is not to suppose they have nothing to offer, nor that they operate as some sort of dictatorship. But it does mean they have power and influence over policy formation, which will have implications for the relationships between the various branches of our constitution that prove unsettling.[31] Crucially, the more political they become, the more the question of 'who voted for you?' becomes necessary.

Summary

Two things stand out in this chapter, namely a sense of chaos within government over how quangos are run, or even defined. The Cabinet Office is supposed to boss these public officials around yet fails to do so, while also being tasked with making things better. This is despite the obvious perverse incentives that dominate quangos and the Cabinet Office itself. They are in perfect harmony on this front. The second is the rebelliousness and resistance to the appointment of independent-minded, publicly-interested unusual suspects to lead our quangos.

2

How many quangos?

Introduction

This chapter gets to grips with establishing how many quangos there are and what the long-term trend is. First, it looks at the numbers employed and the money spent on them. It then presents results of a short survey that tries to establish the extent to which they are well-run. It concludes with evidence to suggest a risk of institutional capture from vested interests as well as exposure to corporate lobbying, that raise questions over transparency and accountability.

How many?

The short answer to this question is, no one really knows for sure. This stems in part from the fact that the definition of a quango is vague and in part because some are permitted to operate outside of the Cabinet Office's purview. The Office for National Statistics (ONS) keeps a list of public bodies which includes 3,163 organisations, although the extent to which all are operational today is hard to discern. Of these, there are 854 central government public bodies and 735 local government public bodies.[32] And according to the government's website, there are 420 'agencies and other public bodies'.[33]

The Cabinet Office keeps a more restricted list of ALBs, which it defines as 'a specific category of public body including executive agencies, non-departmental public bodies, and non-ministerial departments'.[34] Statistics on such organisations are released annually. According to the latest release, there are 295 ALBs. But a report by the National Audit Office (NAO) says there are further 'unclassified bodies' that 'do not fall within the remit of the Cabinet Office's monitoring and review processes'.[35] At the time of writing, the most recently released statistics pertained to 2020. The next round of statistics appears long-overdue.

It is thus difficult to say how many quangos there are, or what is an ALB and what is just a public body for that matter. The sprawling number and lack of knowledge are both symptoms of the same problem, namely governance that grows and grows without knowledge of what it is doing. Nevertheless, Cabinet Office statistics give a picture of declining numbers of ALBs, in line with the Coalition Government's previous promise of a 'bonfire of the quangos'.

According to the most recent Cabinet Office statistics, the 295 breaks down as:

Table 2.1. Classification of arm's length bodies, 2020

Classification of ALB	Number
Non-departmental public body	237
Executive agency	38
Non-ministerial department	20
Total	295

Source: Cabinet Office.

Using publicly available data, it is possible to trace back the number of non-departmental public bodies (NDPBs), a subset of ALBs, encompassing organisations that are advisory, tribunals, or have some executive capacity (not to be confused with executive agencies!), as far as the late 1970s. As seen in Figure 2.1, the number of NDPBs has fallen substantially from 2,167 in 1979. This is down to a large fall in the number of advisory NDPBs. The rate of change appears to sharpen during the Coalition years (2010-15).

However, it is possible that declines may be attributable simply to reclassification. The same NAO report says the decline between 2016 and 2019 was 'in large part driven by the reclassification of bodies and does not reflect a true reduction in the number of bodies delivering across government'. Over that period, we lost 168 ALBs, only this was accomplished by 143 being 'reclassified outside boundary'.[36] Furthermore, the Cabinet Office released a data set called 'Public bodies closed as at 22 August 2012', which is a list of 106 organisations supposedly 'closed'.[37] Downloading the dataset reveals they are merely 'No longer an NDPB' and nothing more. The Civil Service Appeal Board still exists despite being 'closed' in December 2011.[38] The Alcohol Education and Research Council is now an independent charity, despite its 'closure' in July 2012, and described online as 'dedicated to sharing information under government supervision'.[39] Others genuinely do appear to have closed proper, such as the UK Film Council.

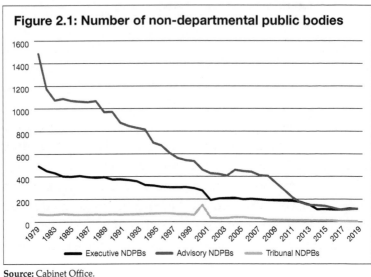

Figure 2.1: Number of non-departmental public bodies

Source: Cabinet Office.

While the number of executive NDPBs has fallen, those that continued became bigger in terms of staffing. While the number of people employed in such organisations fell from around 22,000 in 1979 to 11,000 in 2020, the corresponding numbers *per organisation* were 441 and 923. This would entail a doubling in the number of staff per organisation, consistent with a disbanding of advisory bodies that will naturally be fewer in staff numbers.

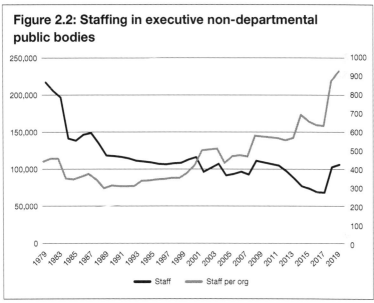

Figure 2.2: Staffing in executive non-departmental public bodies

Source: Cabinet Office.

In terms of expenditure, the amount of money spent on executive NDPBs is at a historic low at £15 billion. In 1970, we spent £30 billion in today's prices. It reached almost £60 billion in 2009 before falling thereafter, despite a blip in 2016. But as seen in the graph below, we spend slightly more on substantially less. In 2020 we spent £150 billion per executive NDPB, up from £60 billion in 1979.

Such figures pertain to a subset of staffing and expenditure and are deployed to give some indication of trends over time based on limited data since historic Cabinet Office releases are limited to disclosures on executive NDPBs. In 2020, the amount of money spent in total on all classified ALBs was £223.9 billion while the number of people employed was 318,714. However, because we cannot say how many quangos there are for sure, equally we cannot say how much they spend or how many they employ.[40]

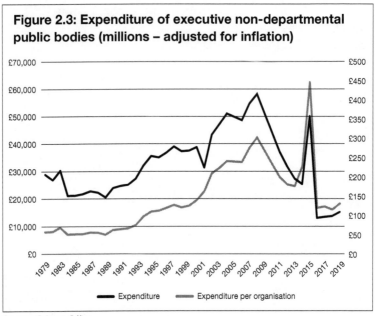

Figure 2.3: Expenditure of executive non-departmental public bodies (millions – adjusted for inflation)

Source: Cabinet Office.

How well run are they?

To try and establish this for the purposes of this report, a series of questions were put to 30 quangos, selected from the Cabinet Office's list of ALBs, as requests under the Freedom of Information Act. All ALBs have something called a 'framework agreement' which outlines its responsibilities and relationship with its sponsoring department. These were supposed to be updated within the last three years,[41] reflecting whatever changes there might be. Thus, Question 1 was,

• When was your framework agreement last updated?

Before introducing any new policy or regulation, government bodies are supposed to carry out regulatory impact assessments.[42] These require a justification of the proposed measures as well as an assessment of the likely costs and benefits. Question 2 was,

• Does your organisation carry out impact assessments before introducing a new policy or regulation?

Governmental bodies should also have registers of interests for senior figures as well as registers of any gifts or hospitality received from third parties. Thus, we have Questions 3 and 4,

• Does your organisation keep a register of interests?

• Does your organisation keep a register of any hospitality received from third parties?

Asking such questions should give a broad measure of the day-to-day functioning of quangos, but would not preclude any objections to their efficacy in meeting their actual objectives. The results of this short survey are presented in the Table 2.2.

As shown, two thirds of those bodies surveyed had updated their framework agreements within the last three years. This is broadly in line with a small sample made by the National Audit Office that found nine out of 12 ALBs that it surveyed had met the three-year target for reviewing their framework agreements.[43] Concerning impact assessments, 11 out of 15 quangos made these before introducing a new regulatory policy. (Note the sample size was restricted to those with a regulatory function.) All bodies surveyed had a register of interests, while nearly all had registers of gifts and hospitality.

Table 2.2. Survey of quangos results

	Framework agreement updated in last three years?	Impact assessments made?	Register of interests?	Register of gifts and hospitality?
Number	19 (66%)	11 (71%)	30 (100%)	28 (93%)
Sample size	29	15[44]	30	30

Source: FOI/Civitas analysis.

The results of this survey would suggest that, on the whole, ALBs are largely well run. The fact that one third are behind in reviewing their framework agreements would suggest a substantial institutional lethargy in a minority of ALBs.

Lobbying and conflicts of interest

One way to look at this is to examine quango's registers of interests and gifts and hospitality received. These were also obtained as part of the same FOI survey. But first, some caveats. All individuals have interests and even conflicts of them, in that in the very least, the private interests of someone may conflict with the general interest of a supposedly public-serving institution. Moreover, any technocratic governmental organisation is going to need technocrats which will have to be recruited from somewhere, most likely business or academia, which will both want more business and more academia. Nevertheless, there are genuine, apparent conflicts of interest that are sometimes quite stark and a cause for legitimate concern within our quangos. This is not to imply wrongdoing but simply to make the point that there is an expectation that public bodies work in the public interest, and that public servants be seen to do so.

Similarly, gifts and hospitality received do not signify in themselves a significantly beneficial government contract won. Far from it. Nor would we expect public bodies not to be lobbied in some sense, since it is right that private interests communicate their needs to those who regulate them, within reason and fairly.

Out of the 30 ALBs as surveyed before, 20 had some signs of potential conflicts of interest. Take for example the National Infrastructure Commission, which was set up in 2015 to 'provide impartial, expert advice and make independent recommendations to the government on economic infrastructure'. Its remit covers: energy, transport, water, waste, biodiversity, and housing.[45] The table below presents some of the potential conflicts of interest.[46] Reading the Commission's declaration of interests, one thing that is most apparent is the extent of capture by the professions, with many of its associates being members of professional associations representing architects, engineers, management consultants, and accountants.

Table 2.3. Selected potential conflicts of interest among members of National Infrastructure Commission

Position	Potential conflicts of interest
Commissioner	Chairman of National Express & shareholder; Board member of Berkeley Homes & shareholder
Commissioner	Director of dRMM Architects; Director of Major Projects Association; Member of Net Zero Buildings Council; Fellow of Royal Institute of British Architects
Commissioner	Chairman of a retail bank in the North East; Chairman of M6 Toll Road; Non-executive director of Northumbrian Water; Fellow of Institute of Civil Engineers
Commissioner	Partner of Meridiam (company specialising in infrastructure projects); Director of Fulcrum Infrastructure Group
Commissioner	Director of Oxford Infrastructure Analytics; Fellow of Institute of Civil Engineers

Source: National Infrastructure Commission.

The nature of the National Infrastructure Commission is technocratic. Some quangos are, however, more ostensibly political. Take the Low Pay Commission, the body that advises the government on the minimum wage, which shows a strong political bias. Five out of nine commissioners are either members of the Labour Party or have been, and a further one is a member of the Liberal Democrats.[47] That is to say, commissioners are predominantly drawn from the political parties more strongly favouring state-sanctioned increases in the minimum limit to be set on wages.

Out of 30 ALBs surveyed, 15 showed signs of having being lobbied, judging by their registers of hospitality and gifts. Take for example the UK Space Agency, which orchestrates and subsidises the British space industry. Since 2019, its senior figures have accepted hospitality from companies such as Airbus, QinetiQ, Jacobs, Lockheed Martin, Virgin Orbit, Orbex, Skyrora, BAE Systems, and Boeing, to name a few.[48] While it is only proper that such an agency seek contacts in the private sector, it is impossible for the general public to know what was discussed or if any advantages stemmed from them.

Summary

It is not clear how many quangos there are. What official figures there are relate to just a subset and it is impossible to say for sure what the current trend is, in terms of their number. Quangos would appear on the surface to be well run but somewhat sluggish. There are also questions about their being open to capture by vested interests and transparency regarding lobbying. There is little point in ministers surrendering control of aspects of governance only for it to be taken up by vested interests. The question of 'arm's length' may very well be not one of 'why?' but 'from whom?'

3

Studies of failure

Introduction

To strengthen the critique of the quango state, this chapter looks at some case studies of quangos, to highlight how and why they might go wrong. Often, when they fail, the effect is spectacular. Note that any given quango may run smoothly internally while still bringing catastrophe to the general public.

SAGE – the rule of the guardians

The Scientific Advisory Group for Emergencies (SAGE) is a committee of scientific advisors which will spring into life in the event of a national emergency. It is tasked with providing the government impartial scientific advice on how to proceed. It has been activated nine times since 2009 in response to natural disasters, nuclear emergencies (Fukushima) and diseases.[49] Its most recent was in response to the Covid-19 pandemic that began in China in 2019 and resulted in national lockdowns here. It has since stood down as the virus lost its potency and the country resumed something akin to normalcy.

Since SAGE is a committee of advisors, and since many quangos are advisory committees, it falls within the remit of this study. That it escapes the usual oversight that accompanies quangos only underlines the point that something went drastically wrong. A committee that was supposed to advise government was, as critics have alleged, dictating policy to it.

SAGE was chaired jointly by the government's Chief Scientific Adviser, Sir Patrick Vallance, and Chief Medical Officer, Sir Chris Whitty. Its membership and the advice it gave, in the form of the minutes of its meetings, were initially withheld from public view, only to be published at a later date. SAGE is basically a list of names, a nomenclature of experts, who can be called upon as necessity dictates. According to its official remit, where risks are known, membership should come from existing governmental scientific advisory groups and 'this pre-defined list should form the starting point for defining SAGE membership.' Where emergencies are unforeseen, 'the SAGE secretariat will need to define SAGE membership'.[50]

Trying to find out who sat on SAGE is a problem as all that is presented on the government website are the names of everyone who ever participated in a SAGE meeting. Including all its sub-groups, they number into the hundreds.[51] Given that it is simply a list, from which advisors can be called upon at whim, it is hard to know if Professor Neil Ferguson could ever have resigned from SAGE, despite a statement that he 'stepped back' from his involvement in SAGE after being caught receiving visits from his mistress in breach of the lockdown rules he advocated for.[52] Certainly, he continued to participate in some form thereafter.[53]

Missing from the list are the known and most vocal scientific sceptics who should have been called upon to advise the government, if only to offer a dissenting minority view. The authors of the *Great Barrington Declaration* (Martin Kulldorff, Sunetra Gupta, Jay Bhattacharya), who advocated shielding for the most vulnerable while eschewing lockdowns,[54] do not appear, nor do sceptics such as Carl Heneghan or Karol Sikora. These are all scientists who took a different opinion, only they were not included within the SAGE list. Should science really exclude dissenting scientific opinion? The answer is no, but this is not science but rather *government science*, and that creates a problem in that it invites conformity and factions. To quote Adam Smith,

> 'People of the same trade seldom meet together, even for merriment and diversion, but the conversation ends in a conspiracy against the public, or in some contrivance to raise prices.'[55]

The accuracy of its advice has been criticised as fear-mongering and based on modelled projections that proved inadequate.[56] Ferguson's estimation that the virus could kill half a million without intervention, is said to have 'spooked' the government into lockdown.[57] The model behind this estimate has been thoroughly criticised, with its application in Sweden being said to have predicted 96,000 deaths, whereas in realty there were just 12,560 – out by a factor of seven. Crucially, Sweden had no formal lockdown.[58]

Moreover, Ferguson had a track record of being ingloriously inaccurate. Ferguson predicted 136,000 deaths from vCJD (mad cow disease) in 2001, when in fact 2,826 died. He predicted in 2005 up to 200 million dead worldwide from bird flu; the actual number was 616. He predicted in 2009 that swine flu would in a 'worst case scenario' lead to 65,000 UK deaths. The actual number was 457. His work also underlay the slaughter of 6.5 million animals in 2001, in response to the outbreak of foot and mouth, which was severely criticised as unnecessary.[59]

But perhaps the most damaging revelations came from Rishi Sunak, then speaking as a former chancellor and candidate for Tory leader. In an interview with Fraser Nelson of *The Spectator*, he divulged some of what went on during the pandemic.[60] As Nelson wrote,

> 'A cost-benefit calculation – a basic requirement for pretty much every public health intervention – was never made. "I wasn't allowed to talk about the trade-off" says Sunak... "The script was: oh, there's no trade off, because doing this for our health is good for the economy."'

In order to justify the lockdowns, the government needed to present them as a scientific policy rather than a political decision. This meant 'elevating' SAGE into a committee with the 'power to decide whether the country would lock down or not.' No comparable forums for discussing the economic and social impacts were provided for, apparently.

Sunak further recounted how a treasury official, a 'lovely lady', would sit in unnoticed on SAGE meetings, who would give him a fuller account of what transpired. From this, he would learn that the 'all-important minutes' would often 'edit out dissenting voices'. *The Spectator* article continues:

> 'Typically, he [Sunak] said, ministers would be shown SAGE analysis pointing to horrifying 'scenarios' that would come to pass if Britain did not impose or extend lockdown. But even he, as chancellor, could not find out how these all-important scenarios had been calculated.
>
> "I was like: Summarise for me the key assumptions, on one page, with a bunch of sensitivities and rationale for each one", Sunak says. "In the first year I could never get this." The Treasury, he says, would never recommend policy based on unexplained modelling: he regarded this as a matter of basic competence. But for a year, UK government policy – and the fate of millions – was being decided by half-explained graphs cooked up by outside academics.'

SAGE's spell was broken in December of 2021, when its analysis that without a further (fourth) lockdown deaths could rise to 6,000 a day was rejected – out by a factor of 20 as it transpired. Sunak solicited advice from Stanford University (where Bhattacharya works) as well as JP Morgan. Relying on observations from South Africa of the Omicron variant, they were able to predict, correctly, that the new wave would not be so dangerous. But the question will remain, why did it take the chancellor to inject this into the scientific/political deliberations, which ought to have been open to it in the first place? Moreover, why was a scientific advisory body of supposed experts promulgating within government ideas and information that obscured the correct course of action from elected politicians like Sunak? This is the exact opposite of what a 'sage' is supposed to do.

What went wrong? According to former Cabinet Secretary Gus O'Donnell, the problem is there was not another committee for SAGE to report to that would balance their advice against economic and social imperatives.[61] If only we could find the right quango! This does nothing to address the problems inherent with SAGE. Ministers deferred responsibility because they were ignorant of science and needed scientific cover for political decisions. In doing so, they empowered *one faction* of scientists, who operated SAGE as a closed shop, protecting academics with a track record of failure as well as groupthink. Future emergencies can avoid this trap by redefining the role of the Chief Science and Medical Officers within future SAGEs as seeking both authoritarian and libertarian proposals, and inviting their proponents to contest their ideas in debate before ministers. They should act as explainers of science to ministers as well as impartial umpires. No scientists should be embedded as the government's favoured scientists.

The Bank of England

The Bank of England is an important case study since it provides a test of the thesis that political independence is for the best. The recent growth in inflation and the Bank's response arguably provide, at the very least, evidence that technocracy is no guarantee of responsiveness to need. As we reach 25 years of its independence, and in the wake of rampant inflation, critics have begun to question its value – with Liz Truss, in her ill-fated leadership campaign, having promised to look at the issue afresh.[62]

The Bank is the central bank of the United Kingdom. It is tasked with providing secure banknotes, regulating UK banks and other financial firms, and keeping the cost of living stable.[63] As part of this latter function, its goal is to ensure inflation rises no more than two per cent each year. Inflation at the time of writing is 10.1 per cent.[64]

The Bank is a public body that is accountable to Parliament. It was granted independence from political control in 1997, giving it the right to set interest rates. This was justified on the grounds that political considerations were getting in the way of setting the right path forward. As Eddie George, the Bank's governor at the time, said, 'we will not be distracted by political considerations. We are doing a technical job'.[65] According to Gordon Brown, the objectives were 'high and stable levels of employment and growth'.[66] The argument went that politicians would be reluctant to raise interest rates, fearing a political backlash, while technocrats, free from democratic restraints, would have the courage to do so if and when necessary.

While welcomed by many, including the City, there were some sceptics at the time. Dianne Abbott MP criticised its independence in the House of Commons, pointing out 'we cannot decouple economic management from politics'[67] and that the empirical record for central bank independence rested on evidenced correlations not causation. In response, Vince Cable MP added that past chancellors had,

'… forced through many painful decisions to bring down inflation, but they always acted too late. They – or rather, their predecessors – should have acted in advance of inflation appearing. That is what a technically-based, independent central bank can do.'[68]

Yet, the Bank has been criticised for being tardy in its response to rising inflation. Timing also weighs heavily against the current governor of the bank, Andrew Bailey, and his emphasis on the Russian invasion of Ukraine as the key causal factor behind rising inflation. As he said, 'I'd challenge anyone sitting here a year, two years ago, to say there will be a war on Ukraine and it will have this effect on inflation'.[69] The Bank's monthly Monetary Policy Report for August 2022 further attributed the rise in inflation to the Ukrainian situation, claiming 'Russia's invasion of Ukraine has led to more increases in the price of gas', before citing as causal, 'higher prices for the goods that we buy from abroad' and 'businesses charging more for their products because of the higher costs they face' stemming from 'higher wages to attract job applicants'.[70] Russia began its invasion of Ukraine in February 2022, causing gas prices to rise, but that does not explain the rise in inflation from 0.4 per cent to six per cent commencing in April 2021.

The Bank can also be criticised for a lack of foresight when, in the summer of 2021, it projected inflation to peak at four per cent. At the same time, it neglected to raise interest rates from their historic low. Bailey described inflation as 'transitory'.[71] Indeed, its forecasting has been consistently off, with the economist Stephen King asking, 'How many times over the past two years has the Bank of England forecast a significant, lasting problem with inflation? The answer is "never".'[72]

Critics of the Bank, such as the economist Tim Congdon, have put forward an alternative argument, that the Bank itself is responsible for the problems it now seeks to solve. Congdon blames the Bank's 'quantitative easing' policy, which is in effect printing money, as the problem.[73] As seen in the graph below, the supply of 'broad' money increased dramatically before coming down again, followed subsequently by the rise in inflation.[74]

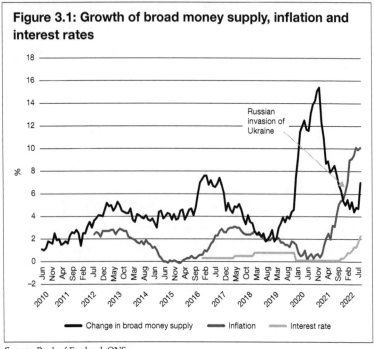

Figure 3.1: Growth of broad money supply, inflation and interest rates

Source: Bank of England, ONS.

Former Bank of England Governor, Mervyn King, has added to this critique, saying recently,

'All central banks in the West, interestingly, have made the same mistake… central banks decided it was a good time to print a lot of money. That was a mistake… We had too much money chasing too few goods.'[75]

That is the definition of inflation. The splurge in quantitative easing that took place during the Covid-19 lockdowns, thus, requires some explanation. According to the economist James Forder,

'It [quantitative easing] was first contemplated as a way to loosen monetary policy when interest rates were effectively zero. There is certainly a case for such policy. In the financial crisis, it became a means of supplying liquidity. Since it was very much a crisis of liquidity, this would seem reasonable.

'But why was there so much more of it in the pandemic? The answer might be that demand had collapsed, so there was, again, a need to find a way to mimic lower interest rates. Yet the government had told people to stay at home and had shut many of the places where they might have spent their money. No "stimulus to demand" was going to change that. The appearance is much more that the case of quantitative easing was to make it cheap for the government to issue its debt.'

As Forder writes, this may be good policy, but it is political policy as the 'unavoidable essential' is that 'government must be responsible for financing its own expenditure'.[76] Indeed, the Bank admits on its website that quantitative easing 'lowers the cost of borrowing throughout the economy, including for government', adding 'but that is not why we do QE'. Instead, 'we do it to support growth and jobs to hit our inflation target'. It is further stated that quantitative easing 'helps to boost spending in the economy and keep inflation at target'.[77]

Forder further points out the politicisation of the Bank in that its *Inflation Report* published in May 2016 was only an assessment of the risks relating to leaving the European Union, without entertaining any of the possible benefits.[78] He notes that the regulatory obligation to write to the chancellor, should the bank deviate from its inflation target, resulted in an exchange of letters that was tame and perfunctory.

At the same time that the Bank has failed to keep inflation below its target of two per cent, it has also expanded its role. According to its website, climate change,

> 'matters to our mission, which is to promote the good of the people of the United Kingdom by maintaining monetary and financial stability. And this puts climate change at the heart of our prudential, financial stability and monetary policy objectives and the way we run our operations'.[79]

It now has its own 'climate objective and goals' which are to 'ensure the macroeconomy, the financial system, and the Bank of England itself are resilient to the risks from climate change and support the transition to a net-zero economy.'

But it has failed on its bread and butter. As well as embracing the net-zero agenda, it published an 'LGBT+ charter' which it encourages other financial institutions to sign up to.[80] It further spent £50,000 on a new 'inclusive' logo, which is practically identical to its last one.[81] Since 2019, it has spent £9,777.60 on Stonewall (the LGBTQ+ Rights campaigning charity) membership and conferences.[82] It has also hosted an 'Investing in Ethnicity & Race' conference and is signed up to the 'Race at Work Charter' run by the charity Business in the Community.[83] All such measures commit the Bank to fostering societal change, far beyond its basic remit, which it is doing very badly at. Indeed, it has recently been criticised for hiring a former civil servant with 'no economic experience' to sit on its board, as she would 'make a strong contribution to improving diversity and inclusion'.[84]

Should the Bank's independence continue? Would politicians be any better? The argument for independence was made on the assumption that politicians would be hamstrung by their own political incentives. However, seemingly independent technocrats have their own incentives and play their own games too. They have also proved the argument of greater nimbleness in responding to inflation to be wrong. Overlooked has been the fact that independence is synonymous with unaccountability. Perhaps this is settled in light of the fact that the Bank's operations could be described as 'independent but cosy'. As John Redwood MP has written,

> 'This is a body owned by the taxpayer, whose Governor is appointed by the government and who reports to both the Chancellor and the Treasury Committee of Parliament. On its website, it tells us that its dominant policy of the last 12 years, printing loads of money and buying bonds was one where it was merely acting as the agent of the Treasury. It is true that successive Chancellors from Alastair Darling to Jeremy Hunt signed off all the bond buying and selling and indemnified the Treasury against the entirely predictable huge losses they will now make on these bonds they bought so badly.'[85]

Politicians are never too far away; arms are only so long. Speaking of which, Liz Truss has recently authored a (qualified) *mea culpa* for her (very) short-lived premiership, published in *The Sunday Telegraph*.[86] Critics were naturally quick to seize on its flaws, pointing out 'you've only got yourself to blame', or words to that effect. But there was one thing in her piece that stood out, namely the role of so-called 'liability-driven investments' (LDIs). These are investments that became popular in the early 2000s that allowed pension funds to free up money so that they could invest in other assets. As Truss says, 'this works when markets are calm but becomes problematic when the price of government bonds falls within a short timeframe'. Truss' argument is that an intervention by the Bank of England the day before her infamous 'mini-budget' created a financial 'tinderbox'. As she writes,

> 'The day before the mini-Budget, the Bank of England raised interest rates by 0.5 per cent, whereas the US Federal Reserve had just announced a third successive rate rise of 0.75 per cent. In addition, the Bank simultaneously confirmed plans for a bond-selling programme. Bond prices fell sharply, putting pension funds under pressure.
>
> 'Dramatic movements in the bond market had already begun, meaning the mini-Budget faced a very difficult environment. Only now can I appreciate what a delicate tinderbox we were dealing with in respect of the LDIs.'

She further claims she and her team were not advised on the matter by officials. As pointed out by Patrick Hosking, who is the Financial Editor of *The Times*,

> 'yields started to accelerate sharply not from the day of the mini-budget but the day before, when the Bank raised [the] base rate and officially pressed the button on quantitative tightening'.

This contradicts the standard story that Truss and Kwasi Kwarteng triggered a collapse in the bond market with an ideological and cockamamie fiscal intervention. Hosking says, 'formally announcing that [the Bank] would start to sell £80 billion of its stockpiled bonds certainly didn't help'. He concluded that,

> 'The Pension Regulator seems to have been so busy encouraging pension schemes to embrace liability-driven investment that it and the Bank omitted to look at what was being created – a gigantic £1 trillion herd, all facing in the same direction.'[87]

Inevitably, 'recollections may differ' for all parties concerned, but if Truss' account is correct then this raises an important constitutional problem. This can be defined as the technocratic wing of governance heaping up problems which the democratic wing carries the can for, and which many partisans and much of the politicised media are only too happy to go along with. This is hardly fair and it seems accountability may have been a one-sided affair.

Questions about the Bank's competence must be asked given that it had been warned about the risks of LDIs[88] as well as the fact that its own pensions scheme worth £5 billion, which until June of last year, was entirely invested in a single Blackrock LDI fund (now down to 80 per cent).[89] As argued by Jon Moynihan, this 'suggests a serious potential conflict of interest concerning the Bank's interventions in the bond markets and of its own employees' pensions'.[90] All this underscores the fact that no one is every truly 'independent' since we all have our own interests. The point of democratic control is to have a check on self-interested elites who may stray too far from the public good, only this is missing for an institution like the Bank of England.

'I' is for Independent – the capture of the IOPC

The Independent Office for Police Conduct (IOPC) exists as the independent regulator responsible for serious allegations of misconduct or criminal offences committed by police officers. Its recent report into the police's handling of sexual abuse of girls in Rotherham, mostly white, largely carried out by gangs of men who are Pakistani in origin and Muslim, was damning. It brought attention onto the IOPC and its limited powers, since no officers have been fired. As Sarah Champion MP wrote in *The Times*, the IOPC can only respond to complaints referred from the police and then 'recommend to the appropriate authority that there is a case to answer'. The appropriate authority will invariably be the police.[91]

It seems the IOPC is as terrifying as any toothless tiger, but there is much more deserving scrutiny. The dogma of the Left suggests that bad behaviour is caused by 'cultures' of racism, misogyny, homophobia, and so forth. These persist in 'canteen culture' and possess individuals to transgress, much like evil spirits. The solution is cultural reform, led by 'experts', who take the form of diversity and inclusion workers or external and ideological consultants such as the LGBTQ+ Rights campaigning charity, Stonewall. See, for example, the recent *Independent Culture Review of London Fire Brigade*, led by Nazir Afzal.[92]

The capture extends to the IOPC, which is signed up to Stonewall, having paid it £15,000 over the last five years. It has two subscriptions, one for England and one for Wales.[93] Its chief investigator in the Charing Cross affair, where officers were found to have sent offensive messages on WhatsApp and Facebook, Sal Naseem, describes himself as 'championing, practicing and speaking publicly about the principles of equality, diversity and inclusion', committed to 'working on initiatives to help the progression of those who are underrepresented in the workforce in the day job and outside of it'.[94]

He sits on the advisory board of Tell MAMA,[95] which collects reports of 'hate crimes' against Muslims, benefiting from data-sharing agreements with the police[96] and government funding.[97] The IOPC has a role in investigating so-called 'super-complaints,' which are complaints into supposed systematic police failures. Only a set list of organisations – government-approved complainers – can make complaints, and this includes Faith Matters, which is the parent organisation of Tell MAMA.[98]

The IOPC submission to Stonewall's Diversity Champions scheme is online.[99] It details its attendance at 'Pride' celebrations, unconscious bias training, and 'LGBT+ staff networks'. It shows how 'LGBT+' activists participated in an IOPC investigation. This echoes the involvement of the National Black Police Association's (NBPA) role in *Operation Hotton* into the Charing Cross scandal, which encouraged forces to work with 'staff associations to identify areas for improvement and embed changes'. In other words, organisations like the NBPA. The IOPC also 'raised money for Stonewall Housing and the Proud Trust during Pride Month'. Rainbow lanyards and 'pronoun badges' are available. Since 2019, the IOPC has paid £42,000 in membership fees to a diversity consultancy named Vercida, plus £4,410 for 'targeted campaigns'.[100]

Its 'Pride LGBTQ+ staff network' supplies it with a 'Glossary of LGBT Terms', a nomenclature of all things gay and trans. It is helpful for those unsure of their 'twinks', 'bears', and 'bottoms'. But it also introduces politically contested ideas into what should be a neutral organisation. For instance, 'sex' is 'assigned' rather than observed at birth. 'Gender' is the 'social construct of being a man or a woman', and not a synonym for 'sex', as is its dictionary definition.[101] 'Transphobia' is defined as 'the irrational fear or dislike of someone who is trans and can include the refusal to accept their gender identity'. Thirty-six per cent of adults disagree that 'a transgender woman is a woman',[102] so would likely be classed as 'transphobes' by the IOPC. Given that it may have to investigate incidents pertaining to the treatment of transgender people by and within the police, this does much to prejudice any outcome. The glossary may seem innocuous but once you dictate the terms, you assume power.

The IOPC has an 'External Stakeholder Reference Group'

(ESRG) which is an advisory board. It includes Stonewall, but also police bodies, charities, and academics.[103] You cannot claim independence and offer privileged positions to vested interests. Minutes of the meetings of the ESRG are unpublished but two copies of its most recent were obtained.[104] They mention 'collaboration' with third parties, in particular the College of Policing, which was supposed, on its inception (2012), to provide training and expertise but is seeking a greater role. It has since received investigatory powers, through the invention of so-called 'super-complaints' and is regarded by its critics as a den of 'wokery.'

It becomes clear that the prize is the IOPC's very independence. Minutes from March 2022 state,

'Feedback from external stakeholders was that the IOPC should be influencing improvements rather than generating them. We should use our unique role of independence to step outside of policing culture to drive and influence change. Stakeholders wanted the IOPC to become a trusted source of information and combat misinformation. There were also calls for us to become a more vocal, visible and powerful independent voice. It was also suggested that VAWG [violence against women and girls] and discrimination should be a priority focus.'

Other minutes speak of the IOPC seeking 'a stamp of trusted recognition, akin to the Queen's royal stamp' in its quest for 'tangible cultural change'. Reading between the lines, this would allow activists to funnel propaganda into the public realm under the guise of neutrality, utilising the *imprimatur* of the IOPC. This is, to an extent, an ideologically-captured institution with limited capacity to hold the police to account. Those that seek to exploit its independence would weaken it further.

The British Business Bank – *Ceci n'est pas une banque*

The British Business Bank (BBB) was first proposed in 2012 by Coalition Government minister Vince Cable. The intention was to consolidate some existing governmental schemes for small and medium enterprises (SMEs), and to increase the supply of finance available to them. The BBB began life within the then-Department for Business, Innovation and Skills, before receiving permission from the EU Commission to begin operation once it had cleared EU rules on state aid. It began its operations properly in 2014. It is not listed as an ALB in the Cabinet Office's statistics but has all the markings of one. According to its website, it is a government-owned business development bank dedicated to making finance markets work better for smaller businesses'.[105] Its corporate structure shows it is sponsored by the Department for Business, Energy, and Industrial Strategy.[106]

While named as a 'bank', its website has the disclaimer that 'British Business Bank plc and its subsidiaries are not banking institutions and do not operate as such.'[107] Nor is it regulated by the Prudential Regulation Authority or Financial Conduct Authority. Instead, it seeks to encourage lending by financial institutions to smaller businesses, by offering part-guarantees.[108] The BBB does not lend or invest directly, but through a network of 'partner' organisations including banks, leasing companies, venture capital funds, and web-based platforms.[109]

According to a report by the National Audit Office, published in 2020, the BBB had made a good start. The report notes the BBB's stated aim is to 'increase the supply of finance available to smaller businesses where markets don't work well.'[110] It found 'the Bank met or exceeded its targets, within the context of a generally benign economic environment'. The 'stock of finance resulting from the

Bank's programmes, including its own funds and private investment' increased by £13.9 billion, with 89,900 businesses benefiting. It is claimed for every £1 the BBB has 'invested', £5.60 of private investment has been 'attracted'.

The flaw in this argument is that the BBB was founded at a time when the finance sector was in chaos in the wake of the financial crisis and subsequent recession. Any positive signs recorded by the BBB may simply be evidence of an effect of the wider recovery. Moreover, we can challenge the suitability of the BBB's mission to lend more. It is easier to lend money than it is to lend it well. The NAO report does nothing to establish if the BBB invests wisely.

As already mentioned, the BBB tends not to lend directly to businesses but rather through a network of 'third-party delivery partners' of which there were 134 in 2020. As the NAO report makes clear, in 2014, the Committee of Public Accounts recommended the BBB 'make clear how much finance is reaching SMEs, how much is paid to third parties and the direct costs, for each programme'. This was accepted by the government, only the data have not materialised. Apparently, 'the Bank considers that to publish such information would reveal sensitive information to delivery partners and weaken its commercial position'. That is all very well, but how can we know if what is in effect a subsidy to the financial sector is spent wisely? How do BBB-backed businesses fare compared to others? The NAO report further noted BBB estimates that between 32 and 65 per cent of loans 'would not have been available without the Bank's programmes', implying a degree of crowding out of private money. [111]

That the BBB's impact may be more limited is underscored by data from the Bank of England on financial institutions' lending to small to medium enterprises. As seen in the graph below, since 2014, the monthly increases in lending have fluctuated around zero, discounting the Covid-19 splurge. The same trend is evidenced in lending to large enterprises, counting against any causal impact of the BBB, in at least sustaining whatever lending there is (Figure 3.2).[112] These data were not included in the NAO report.

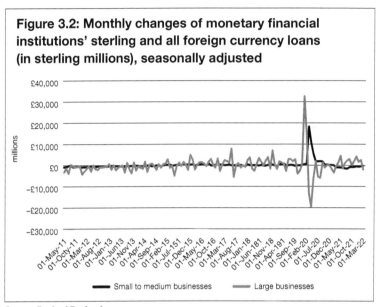

Figure 3.2: Monthly changes of monetary financial institutions' sterling and all foreign currency loans (in sterling millions), seasonally adjusted

Source: Bank of England.

In 2021, Artem Terzyan and Deivis Grochiatskij from Russia and Lithuania, respectively, were jailed for orchestrating a money laundering scam worth £70 million, of which £10 million came from the government's Bounce Back Loans scheme. This was overseen by the British Business Bank and designed to help small businesses that had seen their incomes seize up due to the lockdown. Businesses could take out loans of up to £50,000 from existing creditors that would be backed by the government in cases of default.

According to the BBC, both men 'started fraudulently

claiming Bounce Back Loans in 2020 for the various shell companies they had set up', while *on bail for separate fraud charges*. As pointed out by Angela Eagle MP, that would entail 200 loans made to men who at the time were, at the very least, suspected fraudsters. While grilling bosses from the Treasury and BBB, she raised the possibility of the Bounce Back Loans scheme being 'milked' by Russian organised crime, speaking of a 'bonanza' of fraud.[113]

She is not wrong. Official estimates put the amount lost to fraud at £4.9 billion, or 11 per cent of the value of all loans made under the scheme.[114] A BBC investigation showed how criminals saw the scheme as 'free money'.[115] Paper companies were bought and sold so that more money could be claimed. One source told the BBC, '… to get the maximum £50,000 loan you'd have to put £250,000 turnover… They don't ask for any proof or anything like that.' Another said he had sold about 700 companies, all of which got a Bounce Back Loan.[116]

According to an investigation by the National Audit Office,

'The Scheme facilitated faster lending by removing credit and affordability checks and allowing businesses to self-certify their application documents. As the Scheme progressed, it continued to rely on businesses self-certifying their application details, even as the urgent need for finance reduced. Government ruled out options for additional upfront counter-fraud measures when the Scheme was extended. The impact of prioritising speed is apparent in the high levels of estimated fraud. Counter-fraud activity was implemented too slowly to prevent fraud effectively and the Department's focus is now on detection and recovery of fraudulent loans.'[117]

It has further emerged that the BBB has identified 22,900 Bounce Back scheme 'facilities' which could be 'involved in a case of duplicate loans', meaning loans claimed more than once for the same businesses.[118]

To be fair, the BBB did raise the alarm, but only once so much of the money had already been doled out, while the responsibility for the design of the programme may have rested within the Treasury.[119] Nevertheless, that people cheat is not a revolutionary insight in the field of economics and any loans scheme could easily have been better designed with more stringent counter-fraud measures. It is likely that most of the money will never be recouped and the criminals brought to justice, since the police anti-fraud team has just the capacity to deal with 50 cases per year.[120] At the same time, all those who took out loans legitimately will have to repay them.

The scandal of Covid loan schemes triggered, in part, the resignation of Lord Agnew, who was the treasury minister responsible for counter-fraud. He spoke of 'arrogance, indolence, ignorance' and 'schoolboy errors' in his resignation speech, and over a thousand beneficiaries not even trading at the time they received loans.[121] As he said,

'The oversight by both BEIS and the British Business Bank of the panel lenders of the [Bounce Back Loans Scheme] has been nothing less than woeful. They have been assisted by the Treasury, which appears to have no knowledge of, or little interest in, the consequences of fraud to our economy or society.'[122]

As he makes clear, we now move into the 'dangerous' phase where the banks concerned start to claim on the 100 per cent government guarantees. He added,

'Bizarrely, it took six weeks to get the duplicate check into place, during which time 900,000 loans, or 60 per cent in total, were paid out, bearing in mind that some £47 billion has been paid out.'[123]

He has complained of a 'total lack of transparency' with the then-Chancellor, Rishi Sunak, accused, allegedly, of blocking the relevant data.[124] Indeed, the BBB has an allergy to daylight, with around one third of Freedom of Information requests refused, at least in part, on grounds of 'commercial interests'. It refuses to release the data on the banks involved.[125] It has, however, disclosed that

'BBB practice is to consult with government departments – or indeed other third parties that may be impacted by a proposed FOI disclosure – on the response to FOI requests, where this is relevant.'[126]

The BBB's Covid woes do not end with Bounce Back Loans. The Coronavirus Large Business Interruption Loans Scheme (CLBILS) was a government measure to encourage financial support to larger businesses. Commercial lenders would loan money directly to businesses, backed by an 80 per cent government guarantee. The scheme was developed by the Treasury and the BBB.

Greensill was a financial services company that collapsed in 2021. It had been approved to lend £400 million under CLBILS, by the BBB. Subsequently, the BBB 'became concerned' that Greensill was exceeding the limits of the scheme after it made 'seven loans totalling £350 million' to Gupta Family Group Alliance borrowers, run by the Indian steel magnate Sanjeev Gupta. The BBB then investigated Greensill's lending, before suspending the government guarantee. Greensill, through its administrators, denies any breach of rules. An official inquiry by the National Audit Office concluded that 'had the Bank done more due diligence, including on the loans Greensill claimed it intended to make, it is possible that this situation could have been avoided'. Should the guarantee be successfully claimed, then the taxpayers' bill will be £335 million.[127] (The BBB further runs the Recovery Loan Scheme which has overseen £4.5 billion worth of lending to smaller businesses.)[128]

According to Baroness Wheatcroft, who was one of the BBB's architects, it was 'conceived as a potential solution to growing complaints from smaller businesses about the banks' reluctance to lend, or at least to lend on reasonable terms'. Its purpose lay in 'encouraging new lenders into the market and channelling funds into innovative operators...'[129] However, its role has expanded, with it taking active roles in other matters. In 2021, it announced a 'revised mission and new objective on net zero, reflecting the Bank's commitment to playing an active role in driving a more sustainable economy'. Its mission is now 'to drive sustainable growth and prosperity across the UK, and to enable the transition to a net zero economy, by improving access to finance for smaller businesses'.[130] How improving access to finance for such businesses leads to 'net zero', is unclear.

The NAO report alluded to earlier also shows the BBB taking on two other objectives, these being to 'be the centre of expertise on smaller business finance in the UK, proving advice and support to government', and 'identify and help to reduce regional imbalances in access to finance for SMEs'. As of 2020, it had no official yardsticks for measuring its performance on these two objectives.[131] Moreover, since economic circumstances vary across regions, reflecting natural geographical competitive advantages and disadvantages, there is no reason to expect lenders to be uniformly amenable to lending within regions.

The BBB also runs an 'Investing in Women Code'. This is a 'commitment to support the advancement of female entrepreneurship' which financial institutions can commit themselves to. Signatories commit to:

1. Designate a 'member of the senior leadership team' to be 'responsible for supporting equality in all my organisation's interactions with women entrepreneurs';

2. 'Adopt internal practices that aim to improve female entrepreneurs' access to finance, support and resources;

3. Provide data on its lending and staff and leadership team.[132]

This moves the BBB further beyond its original role, into the realm of social engineering. It simply creates the conditions for more identity politics infrastructure within the private sector. It compels signatories to consider individuals based on their sex, which is what we were all trying to get away from.

The BBB has further intervened in matters of race. In 2020, it was commissioned by the government 'to convene an industry-wide working group on access to capital', which would 'explore the barriers to entrepreneurship and access to finance that impact groups currently marginalised or under-represented across the UK.' This was to feed into the Commission on Race and Ethnic Disparities, which was ultimately responsible for the so-called Sewell Report, after its chair Tony Sewell.[133] Whatever recommendations were made to the Commission are not fully known, but we do know they were rejected by Sewell's commission, with the BBB group moaning to *The Guardian* that it was overlooked for expressing 'inconvenient truths'. One member said,

> 'The reality we discussed, a reality informed by brave research, data, and lived experience highlighted the impact of institutional racism on entrepreneurship. We explained. We offered solutions. But it appears the exercise was always about PR and our work was not convenient for the conclusions they wanted to reach.'

From what can be gleaned from *The Guardian* article, its overtures were likely rejected because they were not very good. '11 evidence-based recommendations' were made, emphasising 'the need for greater access to capital for aspiring and existing minority ethnic entrepreneurs, embedded institutional support and mandatory reporting by employers on ethnic pay gaps'.[134] All this reflects the dogmas of the diversity and inclusion industry, while targeting businesses based on race/ethnicity and not individual merit is only going to fuel bad investments. In any case, the government's Start Up Loans scheme already provides capital and support to those without ready access, and does not target based on race, but is disproportionately taken up by black people.[135] It is administered by the BBB! The case for mandatory ethnicity pay gap reporting has been critiqued elsewhere.[136]

The mission creep does not just extend to net zero and forays into identity politics. The BBB also has a somewhat murky role in national security. The National Security Strategic Investment Fund (NSSIF) is described as 'the government's corporate venturing arm for dual-use advanced technologies' and is a 'joint initiative' between the government and the BBB. In practice, it seems like a fund of money overseen by associates of the intelligence agencies to purchase and develop novel technologies. According to a report in the *Daily Telegraph*, NSSIF exists as a British version of In-Q-Tel, which is the CIA's venture capital fund. NSSIF was set up in 2017 with initial funding of £85 million.

It is not well-known among investors and its employees keep a low profile. According to *The Telegraph*, 'the secretive fund is quickly becoming a vital tool for the security services to access emerging technology built in the UK which could help bolster the country's national security agenda.' It was instrumental in the government purchasing of a 45 per cent stake in OneWeb, rescuing it from bankruptcy. (OneWeb is a company that produces satellites and its purchase came as a surprise to many informed observers.)[137]

The BBB has grown in size as well as remit. In 2014/15 it employed 108 people, rising to 297 in 2018/19. Its expenditure rose rapidly from £9.5 million to £64 million. The value of its assets under management has grown from £2 billion in 2015/16 to £3.3 billion in 2018/19. They are projected to reach £6 billion by 2023/24.[138] It has further subsumed the Start-Up Loans Company and in 2018, 'launched British Patient Capital Limited as a new subsidiary intended to deploy up to £2.5 billion of finance' to support smaller businesses. In 2017 it launched the Northern Powerhouse Investment Fund to provide £400 million to businesses in North England. According to the NAO, the 'Bank's management chose to take on more risk than it was comfortable with' before pulling back.[139] The BBB was scheduled to take over from the European Investment Bank under the 2017 Conservative Manifesto, and would take over the funds that would have gone with it.[140]

It began with a simple goal, to increase the supply of funding to smaller businesses. Data from the Bank of England confirm a negligible impact, despite a positive review from the National Audit Office. The BBB expands both in size and remit, and presides over a fraud scandal worth £4.9 billion of public money that will mostly never be seen again. It usually does not lend directly to smaller businesses, but rather to a network of financiers which it, in effect, subsidises. It will not tell us how such monies are handled, and what proportion makes it through to the intended beneficiaries. The potential for scandal within such dealings, must be substantial. It further indulges in fashionable causes such as radical and divisive programmes to achieve racial and gender equality, plus 'net zero,' only these interventions seem ill-considered, unduly ambitious and dogmatic.

OFWAT – a licence to leak?

Last summer (2022) saw drought hit Britain, with hosepipe bans affecting more than 30 million people following high temperatures and scant rainfall.[141] At the same time as people were not having enough water, three billion litres are lost through leakage each year. Expressed as a fraction of the daily demand for water, that is 20 per cent.[142] Water companies are also criticised for pumping sewage into waterways,[143] while at the same time, making £2.8 billion in profits in 2021.[144]

OFWAT, also known as the Water Services Regulation Authority, is a non-ministerial department, responsible for regulating water companies – with its role including covering leakage. Figures show the amount of water lost to leakage has remained roughly constant over the last 20 years.[145] OFWAT claims that leakage is being reduced by around 11 per cent, but this is only since 2018.[146] Between 1994 and 2000, leaks fell by 36 per cent, but afterwards by just eight per cent.

According to the Angling Trust, the period of stagnation coincides with a change in OFWAT policy that the Trust claims amount to a 'licence to leak'. Under its 'economic leakage level' rules introduced in 2002, 'leakage plans put forward by the industry would only be approved if the value of the water leaks outweighed the cost of repairing those leaks'.[147] Prior, 'strict targets' were imposed (1995) which led to 'significant reductions in leakage levels'. Targets were reintroduced in 2019, when leakage began to fall once more. The Trust notes many water companies met OFWAT standards during the 2000s despite no improvements in the amount of water lost, implying its expectations were too low.[148] According to a report in *The Daily Telegraph*, since 2012, 19 companies have missed their targets on leakage but only one enforcement action has taken place.[149]

The Angling Trust further criticises OFWAT for getting in the way of building new reservoirs, with none opened since 1991. While OFWAT claims this is not such an issue since demand is falling,[150] it seems there has been a considerable lack of attention on the eventuality that we might need to save for a rainless day, despite the climate change political agenda. According to Stuart Singleton-White of the Angling Trust, '… the reality is OFWAT are complicit in our broken water sector and seem to be acting as an apologist for a situation that is bears responsibility for creating'.[151]

At the same time OFWAT has the standard full gamut of diversity and inclusion schemes, including a 'bespoke EDI learning and development programme', unconscious bias training, 'elephant in the room' workshops, 'TinyTalks', reverse mentoring, and 'Outside in Talks'. The latter are a programme of talks from external speakers who 'share their lived and professional experiences of diversity'.[152]

The names of the presentations given under this programme were obtained by Freedom of Information request from OFWAT; names of speakers were withheld but where an organisation was involved, details were provided. In truth, most of the talks had something to do with water or environmental impact. However, some caught the eye as being potentially highly ideological, concerning politically contested matters, and having absolutely nothing to do with water. They tend to fit a pattern of the three big manias that captivate the *bourgeois* political left, these being net zero, diversity and inclusion, and mental health. They are presented in the table below.

The problem with the politicisation of public institutions is that they begin to restrict the room for the dissent of free individuals, since we must all navigate our way through them at some point in our lives. The speaker giving the talk on 'Celebrating Trans Women' was paid £400 to do so.[153]

Table 3.1. Selected presentations from OFWAT's 'Outside in Talks' programme

Title of talk	Organisation giving talk	Month & Year
Discriminatory pricing – exploring the 'ethnicity penalty' in car insurance	Citizens Advice	Jul-22
Celebrating Trans women		Apr-22
Being deaf is my super power	AB Agri	Jan-22
Serious games for serious challenges		Dec-21
TalkTalk & Net Zero	TalkTalk	Dec-21
Rewilding Britain – the story so far	Professor Alastair Driver	Oct-21
Translating ambition into action for our climate and environment	The Institute of Environmental Management and Assessment (IEMA)	Jul-21
Diversity & Inclusion	United Utilities	May-21
Cars that wee (podcast)	National Grid	May-21
Mental health support (podcast)	Money and Mental Health Policy Institute	May-21
Race, diversity and inclusion (podcast)	British Water	May-21
The biggest Arts funder in the world (podcast)	The Arts Council	May-21
To inclusivity and beyond (blog)	Fair by design	Mar-21
Decarbonisation challenges in the water sector – Areas to consider for PR24 and beyond	Mott Macdonald	Feb-21
Money and Mental Health Policy Institute	Money and Mental Health Policy Institute	Jan-21

Source: OFWAT.

The DVLA

The Driver and Vehicle Licensing Agency (DVLA) is responsible for providing driving licenses, vehicle registration, and collecting Vehicle Excise Duty. In 2021, it issued 12.5 million driving licences and collected over £7 billion. Yet, it came in for criticism during the Covid-19 lockdowns as applications went unprocessed and a backlog built up. According to the website Heycar, drivers are still 'waiting up to six months', mostly for paper applications. The waiting list is thought to number around 800,000 – with almost 40 per cent from drivers with medical conditions. The number of medical driving licence applications awaiting a decision has increased from 200,000 in March 2021, to 336,000 a year later.[154] Needless to say, the delay prevents people from getting on with their lives.

What went wrong? Data were obtained from the DVLA under the Freedom of Information Act that show the number of paper applications processed as a percentage of the number of paper correspondence received.[155] As seen in the graph overleaf, this ratio plummets around April 2020 when the first lockdown was imposed, recovers in September of the same year, only to fall away again at the time of the second lockdown, before recovering to a healthy level around June 2020 that has persisted ever since.

The declines in paper applications processed coincides with the shares of DVLA workers physically present within its centre in Swansea. As seen in Figure 3.3, the available data show paper applications troughing in April 2020, at the same time that just seven per cent or workers were on site. Both measures rose only to fall in unison as further lockdowns were imposed.[156]

According to a report from the National Audit Office, 'DVLA's ability to process paper-based applications was reduced during the Covid-19 lockdowns as fewer staff were able to work at its site in Swansea'. It found procedures for processing paper applications were not possible under conditions of working from home, and that many workers had caring responsibilities, while 1,050 were classed as 'vulnerable' with underlying health conditions putting them at greater risk from the virus (c.16 per cent). Some of the delay could further be attributed to 'official guidance' advising GPs to 'pause requests for medical information from DVLA and prioritise work essential for maintaining public health', as well as strike action between April and August 2021. Apparently, a modelling exercise was undertaken:

> 'through the exercise DVLA understood that staff being off site would lead to backlogs in paper-based licence applications, but it did not anticipate the level of sustained disruption from Covid-19 restrictions on its ability to process paper-based applications at its main Swansea site.'[157]

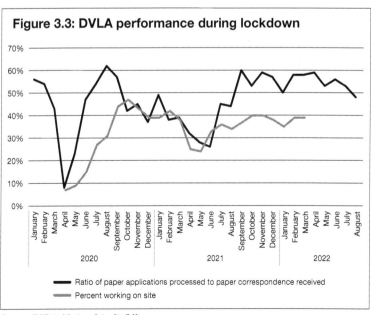

Figure 3.3: DVLA performance during lockdown

Source: DVLA, National Audit Office.

As a consequence, complaints from the public are growing, from 4,300 in 2019/20 to 32,000 in 2021/22.[158] Backlogs in getting licences to people are not just a problem for individuals but also restrict the country's economic activity, and became acute with shortages of lorry drivers, as witnessed in 2021.[159] To be fair, it is hard to plan for an unpredictable pandemic, and contingency plans might fall better within the remit of the Department for Transport. Yet, there is the feeling that DVLA' s expert-led response (N.B. the presence of 'modelling') lacked basic common sense as well as sufficient foresight. You do not need a mathematical model to tell you that with hardly anyone on site, no one will be there to read papers. Why were its workers not prioritised as 'key workers' and how come so many are so disproportionately unhealthy?

The DVLA's latest annual report shows its leadership receiving performance-related bonuses for their work that encompasses the pandemic years, as detailed below. All those mentioned receive basic salaries between £75,000 and £130,000 per year.[160]

Table 3.2. Performance-related bonuses of DVLA executive board members.

Job	Bonus 2021/22	Bonus 2020/21
Chief executive	£5,000 to £10,000	£10,000 to £15,000
HR and estates director	£5,000 to £10,000	£0 to £5,000
Commercial director	–	£0 to £5,000
Operations and customer service director	£0 to £5,000	£5,000 to £10,000
Strategy, policy, and communications director	£5,000 to £10,000	£0 to £5,000
Chief technology officer	£0 to £5,000	£5,000 to £10,000

Source: DVLA.

Sport England – funding sport and more

Some quangos act as funders, doling out millions of pounds of public money each year. One such example is Sport England, established in 1972 as The Sports Council. This financial year, it handed out almost £460 million and over £4 billion since 2009/10 (not accounting for inflation). This money comes from the National Lottery and the Exchequer.[161]

While this undoubtedly funds many worthwhile sporting pursuits, inevitably the money tends to fund other things too. Some organisations that are politically vocal or ideological may put on some sporting functions, thus making them eligible for funding from Sport England. But there is no such thing as money for one thing and money for another in your bank account. By backing such organisations' sporting efforts, Sport England allows them to increase their role, attract more affiliates, and their prestige in the wider community and thus their political reach.

Consider the example of the charity Maslaha, which first received £9,100 in 2015/16 for a project to provide fencing for Muslim girls. Then in 2018/19, for the same project, it received £65,933; then in 2019/20 it got £11,000, before £141,875 in 2020/21 – over a quarter of a million pounds in sum. That is a lot of money for fencing Muslim girls, for whom sports are provided for within schools like anyone else. It would be on top of whatever was received from Comic Relief and Google, listed also as sponsors for the same programme on the Maslaha website.[162]

There, it is explained that 'every school that works with the initiative receives ten weeks of fencing sessions alongside immersive and creative Maslaha workshops, exploring identity, self-expression and challenging stereotypes'. Participants include 'exciting artists', filmmakers, and 'theatre practioners'.

Maslaha is a charity that advocates for Muslims. While moderate, its work takes into account issues beyond sport, including gender, education, criminal justice, and health. It publishes reports and its views can be contentious. For example, it claims Muslims experience discrimination in the courts, that education has to be 'socially and culturally relevant', and provides 'resources that combine religious and medical information which help communities to take control of their own health'.[163] It also provides highly ideological 'anti-racist' training for schools that claims 'thousands of Muslim children' have been 'wrongfully referred' under the government's PREVENT programme.[164] There is the suspicion that the sum of all this is to fuel undue narratives of victimhood as well as encourage segregation. All nothing to do with sport.

Now consider Migrants Organise, an advocacy group for immigrants which received £6,000 from Sport England to run a health and fitness class for women.[165] It defines its work as 'organising is an approach to social and political change...' It runs campaigns to, among other things, grant immigrants access to the NHS.[166] It campaigns directly against the government's Rwanda policy.[167] Again, all this has nothing to do with sport.

Another organisation funded by Sport England and opposing the Rwanda policy is Voice4Change England.[168] It has received grants worth £256,872 in both 2020/21 and 2021/22, rising to £333,934 in 2022/2023. These were for 'sport participation and capacity building' and came out of Sport England's 'Covid-19 Tackling Inequalities Fund'.[169] For much of the time period in question, the only sport available to most was jogging, due to the lockdowns. Voice4Change England is a grant-making body in its own right.[170] Judging from its website, its often produces comment on political matters that have little to do with sport.

There are also examples where public money is being used to subsidise the private charity of those swimming in cash. Consider the Premier League Charitable Fund, the charitable wing of football's Premier League. Since 2013/2014, it has received over £8.7 million from Sport England. Yet the Premier League made a profit of £138 million in 2021.[171] Even its bad players make millions, so why is the public purse funding their supposed generosity?

On the whole, Sport England funds sport. Yet there is an apparent naivety in how some allocations are made. Often, we are seeing public money going to organisations that advocate and provide for just a fraction of the public, fuelling segregation as well as making contentious political contributions, in opposition to the elected government.

The journalist and former table tennis player Matthew Syed has written lately about Sport England, pointing to wider problems than simply poor funding decisions. He writes,

'As a former professional sportsman I have watched with fascination the attempt by the state to achieve a laudable aim: increase the number of British people active in sport... my sense is that as the number of bureaucrats expanded at Sport England — the body set up to allocate billions to create a leaner, fitter Britain — the vitality of grassroots sport declined. The warning signs were obvious early on as coaches gamed the funding system set up by the quango, bribing kids to sign on to their programmes so they could obtain more subsidies. One said: "It was a gravy train."'

'We would later discover that more than 34 per cent of the budget was allocated to administrative overheads. We also learnt that many of the facilities set up at public expense were grievously underused. Meanwhile, the labyrinthine funding "landscape" invented by Sport England to justify the hiring of yet more officials was sucking ever more time from people working on the front line. I remember in the build-up to 2012, when almost all conversations were about "whole sports plans" and almost none about "inspiring more exercise".'

He continues to add that the policy failed and

'the number of people hitting the target figure of three sessions of sport a week didn't increase at all; indeed between 2012 and 2016 it declined, despite the supposed "catalyst" effect of the Olympics.'

Pointedly, he asks, 'Why would we expect a group of bureaucrats in central London to transform the behaviour of people in Newcastle and Newquay?' This perhaps goes to the heart of the fallacy of *quango thinking*, namely elitists trying to improve the behaviour of people they have not met and never will. Syed continued,

'The most fascinating thing, however, is what happened next. Was Sport England disbanded? On the contrary: the quango moved the goalposts. It altered its "target" from the number engaged in three sessions of sport a week to the number engaged in general exercise, such as jogging or walking, which had been rising anyway and had nothing to do with Sport England. Needless to say, ministers were too busy to notice the gerrymandering taking place under their noses, and whenever it was mentioned, Sport England produced a blizzard of statistics to blur what was going on. I couldn't help thinking of the words of Gerald Ford: "One of the enduring truths ... is that bureaucrats survive."'

As Syed points out, adult participation in sport declined after the 2012 Olympics, while Sport England does not know what happened to £1.5 billion of grants it paid out, according to the Public Accounts Committee.[172]

The Climate Change Committee

The Climate Change Committee (CCC) is a non-departmental public body sponsored by the Department for Business, Energy, and Industrial Strategy (BEIS). It is a statutory body, meaning it is defined in legislation, in this case the Climate Change Act 2008. Originally it was set up as the Committee on Climate Change, but changed its name to the Climate Change Committee soon after, at a cost of £20,000. Its remit as defined in legislation is to provide advice to the government on the targets for carbon emissions and carbon budgeting and the extent to which they are met.[173] The latter are legally-binding restrictions on the 'total amount of greenhouse gases the UK can emit over a 5-year period.'[174]

It is chaired by Lord Deben (former Conservative environment minister John Gummer) and its chief executive is Chris Stark. Deben is paid £36,000 per year for 36 days work. If he worked a full working year, he would be paid £255,000.[175] Stark is paid £140,000 per year.[176] The committee itself is composed largely of academics, while it employs a small administrative staff. It has a budget of £5.4 million per year.[177]

Critics point out that the CCC has expanded beyond its legal remit, taking on the role of a prominent government critic. They point to its advocation of the 'net zero' strategy which takes it beyond advising the government into setting the agenda. Annabel Denham of the Institute for Economic Affairs (IEA) points out that the government adoption of the net zero target was undertaken without parliamentary scrutiny because they deferred instead to the CCC's assumed expertise. She says that 'detailed economic analysis on net zero pathways was absent' and the CCC's sums were only published 'long after the legally binding target had been legislated'.[178]

The CCC's self-appointment from government advisors to state-backed critics of the democratic government can be seen in its 2022 *Progress Report to Parliament*, which notes the government's net zero strategy but that 'important policy gaps remain'. It further weighs in on economic policy in that 'action to address the rising cost of living should be aligned with Net Zero' and that 'there remains an urgent need for equivalent action to reduce demand for fossil fuels to reduce emissions and limit energy bills'.[179] These are policy positions put forward by a public body set up supposedly to provide merely advice on how best to set targets. It is now assuming the role of governmental opposition, only under the guise of the detached and impartial expert. However, it pays none of the costs met by opposition MPs that come with seeking public approval at the ballot box.

In fact, the same document makes 327 policy recommendations to the government that increase green regulations and in sum shift the economy towards decarbonisation. It encourages consumers away from eating meat, towards electric vehicles and increased recycling. Because the climate encompasses literally everything, the CCC's chair has criticised attempts to reduce the government's aid budget.[180] The Committee has also dallied in policy matters relating to health and finance, having 'expert advisory groups' on these areas.

Its health group was chaired by Sir Michael Marmot of University College London, recently made a Companion of Honour in the New Years' Honours List of this year (2023) – the country's highest honour. Its report, *Sustainable Health Equity: Achieving a Net Zero UK,*[181] contains a set of policy recommendations that are ambitious to the point of being utopian in its approach. For instance, it calls for 'a wider range of national and local powers to shape food systems and combine these with the resources and statutory duties to support the transition to healthier and more sustainable diets.'

Private car ownership 'does not constitute behaviour change towards more active and inclusive forms of travel' and we shall need 'urban planning models that encourage localised amenities' and 'road space reallocation and holistic behaviour change', through 'flexible traffic control measures that are monitored and enforced.' It calls for 'actions to make four-day working weeks a realistic option' and a 'minimum income standard', based on the vague principle of 'circular economies'. It explicitly seeks a more egalitarian society.

On publication, Chris Stark, who is a public servant and whom no one voted for, said, 'I really welcome this important report'.[182] Yet a cursory reading reveals it to advocate radical societal upheaval, dictated by elites who tell you what to eat and how to travel, and whose first victim is individual liberty, with prosperity next up. Why does the CCC act as think tank for the development of this new strain of environmentalist socialism?

Concerning its engagement with private energy companies through to renewables organisations, clues can be gleaned from looking at its disclosures on gifts and hospitality. The table below details a selection of its members' engagements.[183] While the monetary values are reasonable, particularly estimates of £25 for dinner, the greater concern is that this is privileged access to an influential public body that is supposed to be independent, the content of which goes unrecorded. This is not to imply impropriety but to flag the extent to which the committee is exposed to outside interests.

Table 3.3. Hospitality received by members of the Climate Change Committee

Date	Freebie	Estimated value	Offered by	Notes
2015	Lunch	£25	Energy UK	A trade association for the energy industry
2015	Lunch for 2	£35 per head	Dong Energy	Now known as Orsted, a Danish energy company and 'global leader in offshore wind'
2017	Wimbledon tickets	£200	BP	Energy company. From its website, 'We want to help the world reach net zero and improve people's lives'
2018	Dinner	£25	Macquarie Group	From its website, 'a global financial services group' operating in 'renewables development'
2018	Awards dinner	£40	ADE	The Association for Decentralised Energy, 'the leading trade association for decentralised energy, representing more than 130 interested parties'
2018	Dinner for 6	£35 per head	Wales and West Utilities	Gas suppliers
2018	Dinner	£25	Energy Institute	From its website, 'the chartered professional membership body for people who work across the world of energy. Our purpose is creating a better energy future for our members and society by accelerating a just global energy transition to net zero.'
2019	Dinner	£25	Shepherd and Wedderburn LLP	From its website, a law firm 'at the forefront of innovation in all the key sectors of the economy' including 'our work with Scotland's first tech unicorn and on landmark clean energy projects.'
2019	Lunch	£25	Renewable UK	From its website, 'RenewableUK members are building our future energy system, powered by clean electricity... We support over 400 member companies...'

Date	Freebie	Estimated value	Offered by	Notes
2019	Lunch	£25	Green Investment Group	Part of Macquarie. From its website, 'Our mission is to accelerate the green transition.'
2019	Dinner	£30	Aurora Energy Research	Consultants, 'independent thought partners challenging beliefs, assumptions and strategies, and influencing government policy and the wider energy discussion.' Offers market advice pertaining to energy, boasting of its 'close proximity to markets and clients' that 'gives our analysis the information edge for major investment, strategic and policy decisions.'
2019	Dinner	£25	Carbon Trust	Consultancy. From its website, 'We are your trusted, expert guide on the route to Net Zero...'
2019	Dinner and theatre (the Globe)	£50	Orsted	Formerly Dong Energy
2019	Lunch	£25	Madano	From its website, '... we provide specialist communications support to companies and organisations in the energy and environment sectors'
2019	Burns Supper	£25	EDF Energy	Energy company 'busy building Britain's own wind, nuclear and solar energy supply'
2020	Wine	£50	Burges Salmon LLP	Law firm with, according to its website, 'climate change law expertise', including 'regulatory compliance', 'climate change litigation', and 'funds and investments'

Source: Climate Change Committee

The Climate Change Committee has also been criticised for apparent conflicts of interest held by some of its members.[184]

As we have seen, the CCC has evolved far beyond its envisioned and statutory role of advising government into one of setting the policy agenda and playing the critic. It sees fit to pronounce on anything and everything, yet is exposed to vested interests that undermine confidence in it. The more 'green' policies, the more they benefit.

Matters are made worse in that the course taken by the CCC may not be the correct one. Victoria Hewson of the IEA has authored a critique of the CCC, titled *Hot* Air, pointing out a lack of transparency and also apparent conflicts of interest. She notes that UK carbon emissions were falling before the CCC came into existence and that they amount to a negligible share of global emissions. We have a good track record of meeting targets, yet for the CCC, it is never enough. Hewson further criticises it for an almost obsessive focus on reduction of emissions at the expense of adaptation to climate change. This amounts to punishing consumers, while ignoring the possibility that action is more needed in other countries, most notably China. As she writes, its forays into policy recommendations 'will be used for political and legal leverage by activists and vested interests who wish to advocate particular policies'.

The report's most troubling conclusion is that the very creation of an 'expert' committee of technocrats, supposedly independent, serves only to undermine the democratically elected government that is supposed to make decisions.[185] That the net zero target was adopted into legislation without debate and will prove extremely costly, exposes the stifling effect of technocracy. As Hewson notes, there are 'rational and reasonable concerns about current policies' but such views are not entertained by the CCC.

Summary
Throughout this series of less-than-edifying case studies, we can witness the themes of: failing on your fundamental objectives; excessive ambition; lack of foresight; institutional capture by vested interests; naivety; politicisation; and expert-

led interventions that go wrong. If we measure up these case studies against the following principles of governance to which the organisations in question should be signed up to, we find them wanting in the following ways:

- *Remits should be well defined*: Quangos lack a clarity of purpose with mission creep common. They struggle to stay within their assigned remit and go beyond whatever competencies they have already within themselves.

- *Appointments should be balanced and based on competency*: Organisations like SAGE and the CCC are calling the shots on fundamental matters, yet are staffed with like-minded individuals leading to insular (self-serving) groupthink and the production of 'government science.' Increasingly we are seeing immutable characteristics being at stake in making appointments, despite already existent defensible levels of diversity, when the argument always went that things like race and sex had nothing to do with competence and we were trying to get away from them mattering.

- *Clarity of reporting on performance and meeting of objectives*: Quangos tend to lack any clear limits as to what is good or bad, with the BBB presenting an example of governance without evidence of efficacy. Where reporting occurs, it may be obscure or minimal and left too late, with failures coming to attention of the media or parliament only when things get spectacular.

- *Accountability*: There is a sense that accountability amounts to going through the motions, with a grilling for bosses from parliament from time to time, a negative report from the National Audit Office, and then business as usual. Ambiguous governance arrangements may serve to shield quangos from scrutiny. While ministers are ultimately responsible, it is the inestimable leeway that comes from the 'arm's length' relationship that may prove damning. Recall that Lord Agnew felt the best course of action in his role as a government minister was to resign.

- *Responsibility*: The problem with the 'arm's length' relationship is that the quango boss has an incentive to pass the buck to the minister, who, in turn, has an incentive to offload responsibility onto others.

- *Transparency & openness*: Interested external parties are reliant on annual reports, media, parliamentary hearings and so forth. To know what really goes on takes Freedom of Information requests, but this takes a skill, while organisations such as the BBB are inclined to resist such overtures. Moreover, there exist few with the time and resources necessary to gain access within, or sufficient knowledge of how they work.

- *Addressing conflicts of interest*: While formal rules exist, these sometimes seem woefully inadequate.

- *Integrity*: What rules there are and standards of openness and accountability, including the Nolan Principles of public life, should ensure well-intentioned, public-spirited servants, yet that does not always become apparent. This can be traced back, theoretically, to the problem of 'arm's length,' in that no one is in charge with the perverse incentives that stem from spending other people's money happy to fill the vacuum.

Conclusion – who rules?

This paper is not arguing that quangos should be dispensed with in their entirety, but rather that the assumption should be one in favour of democratically elected oversight through ministers and parliament. If Brexit proved anything it is that our political class is too often out of touch with the public. If public bodies are to deliver on the democratically expressed will of the British people it will require more public appointees who reflect this outlook and far fewer who are at odds with the priorities of the public.

There are two arguments for quangos – that they provide technical competence over matters that require little political direction, for example issuing drivers' licences and so on, and that we need their independence in order to provide regulatory functions that extend to regulation of governance itself. As evidenced in this report, these arguments are somewhat on the back foot, with independence no guarantee of competence, while surely it is the job of parliament and the courts to regulate government? In many instances, the insistence on independence will be illusionary.

In the course of this study, several themes emerged. Quangos are ill-defined, we don't know how many there are for sure. They are expensive and employ a lot of people. While supposedly 'independent' they are actually run by technocrats with their own interests and incentives, as well as a lesser degree of accountability than an elected politician. Technocrats may earn more money than elected politicians, but the institutions they lead are prone to capture, both through vested interests and ideological fads, as well as group think. Our discussion around them is dogmatic and assumes they are necessary. Technocratic rule is no guarantee of competence – quangos may run well from day-to-day but are capable of extraordinary mishaps. While they are critiqued for a lack of accountability and responsibility, they are never too far away from ministerial direction, meaning their existence serves to let politicians of the hook, decreasing their accountability as well.

Perhaps the chief concern is that when political independence is offered by elected politicians, it is gladly accepted only to be abused. Liberal or democratic ideals are replaced with new political ideas that view public institutions not as servants of the people, but sites for the control of their behaviour, either through imposing new social rules or dreaming up polices that are given a free pass by parliament on the assumption these are technical decisions by those who know best, not political decisions made by political actors.

Our problem is a question of *who rules* – is it elected politicians or 'experts'? The preponderance of advisory groups would testify to the fact that underlying so much of *official quango thought* is what the American scholar Thomas Sowell calls the 'unconstrained vision.' This worldview or set of assumptions contends that human beings can be improved through guidance from the most capable individuals. The opposing 'constrained vision' sees them as 'tragic' in the sense of the Greek tragedies; that they have inescapable flaws that are constant throughout history. The former would encourage innovations in governance with more and more quangos posited to take on limitless ambitions in pursuit of perfection.[186]

Advisory bodies

Consider the example of the so-called Social Mobility Commission which humbly aims to 'create a United Kingdom where the circumstances of birth do not determine outcomes in life', as though this were anything other than extremely ambitious.[187] Afterall, how do you escape bad parents? But this was not enough for some. In 2018, Conservative MP Robert Halfon, in his capacity as chair of the parliamentary Education Committee, called for an extension of the Commission's role:

> '...the Commission must have real teeth. First, it should have responsibility to publish social justice impact assessments on all government policies. Second, it should have the power to actively advise on social justice issues rather than at just the request of ministers as currently. And third, the commission must be given more resources and powers.'[188]

This was rejected by the government; had it passed it would have seen the Commission renamed the 'Social Justice Commission' with the power to sway the elected government over all matters of policy as well as supplanting parliament.[189]

This is an example of the kind of ambition that lurks behind quangos – where the officials would take their vision substantively if they got their way procedurally. Note that these proposals were put forward by elected politicians, which speaks volumes as to their faith in the political institutions we have and that exist as solutions to past political problems, chiefly unbridled political power in the form of the monarchy as it was. Halfon's words testify to the collusion between officials and politicians and they are a precise example of the unconstrained vision.

We should question why it is we need so many advisory bodies and 'commissioners' to advise government when that is exactly the role of parliament and there are many organisations, including our largest charities, regularly providing commentary and advice. There is no shortage of research produced by organisations with an interest in advising (or lobbying) government. These advisory bodies should be abolished.

Reforming the quango state

Instead, we should embrace the constrained vision, namely that all branches of governance should exist to serve the people not improve them, acting as restraints on their behaviour if necessary but also subject to those on their own functions. The current situation is unacceptable, as evidenced by the Cabinet Office's inability to get to grips with the quango state. Ultimately, the greatest restraint on quangos should be a more limited ambition. By all means deliver services like licencing of goods and vehicles (please do!), but give up on any attempts to improve people through intensive ultra-reformist public programmes, well beyond democratic consent.

In terms of practical considerations, we might do well to consider the following reasonable steps for what might be done better:

- The Cabinet Office should be stripped of its responsibility for overseeing quangos, retaining merely an administrative role that would include publishing comprehensive statistics on the number of public bodies and their take up of public resources. This register should be updated regularly and placed before parliament with an annual report on expenditure of all quangos to support public debate.

- Government needs to get a grasp of how many quangos there are, with a view to closing those that offer no benefits to the general public. To identify those for closure, it should look for signs of institutional capture, excessive ambition, recency, and costly mistakes.

- Parliamentary accountability should be maximised, with many areas brought back under ministerial control. Most major public bodies, where they are explicitly non-judicial or for some other special reason – should all be more closely under the control of government departments, and civil servants responsible to ministers. Consideration should be given to senior departmental officials chairing these bodies where possible to bring them closer to ministerial accountability.

- Select committees should be given greater responsibility and resourcing to hold quangos to account. Select committees should be required to pay attention to new appointments and strategic planning matters to ensure that priority and delivery match the expectations of the electorate.

- Quango bosses should be held to account at the most fundamental level, which means they can be fired for failure. Pay should be performance-related. There should be regular, scheduled public hearings led by MPs for quango bosses, including questions from journalists. Select committee hearings should go as far as to recommend removal for gross incompetence.

- Advisory committees should be disbanded. Instead, civil servants should be tasked with soliciting advice from across the full range of civil society, for ministers to consider and decide upon their merits. The state should not have embedded experts.

- The elected government needs to consider from first principles, the argument for independence and seek to exert democratic control over governance as much as possible.

All this follows from the democratic principle that we should be governed as much as possible by elected members of the public and that the promised goods of technocratic independence have not materialised. At the same time, a vested interest that sees more of itself as the solution to all problems most certainly has. We need greater accountability over the quango state, as well as reduction, and this will be achieved by greater scrutiny and balance from the democratic elements of our constitution.

Parliamentary select committees

Our unique model of parliamentary democracy rests on MPs in the House of Commons, who above all else are elected and form the centrepiece in the modern, democratic process. The electorate have a special kind of direct input, having elected specific MPs from each constituency. Parliament and its scrutineer MPs and select committees therefore are only able to ensure a meaningful sort of representative government because MPs serve as 'a democratic cockpit of the nation' in the delivery of some agreed-upon common goods. It is a gross misuse of its reputation as a chamber of reasonable debate to decide on government and law when it voluntarily surrenders that obligation for some other superior commitment. Examples would be instructions from some groups of civil servants who believe they have a better sense of ideas, public bodies who devise 'guidance' in the absence of ministerial instruction or agreement, or even through the decisions of a few advisers unconnected to the elected parts of the constitution. To sidestep the process of debate and votes in parliament, or to deliberately cancel scrutiny or debate in the knowledge that society (or some parts of its population) might well disagree with the policies of some new preferred external quango, should be considered well out of bounds.

Parliament should be able to debate the total number of quangos and expenditure each year following publication of a report from the Cabinet Office laid before parliament. This report should provide an accurate reflection of the number of bodies and what they are responsible for as well as estimates for expenditure. Parliament should then be able to approve expenditure.

Select committees already scrutinise ALBs through accountability hearings and pre-approving senior appointments, although these are only advisory and this should continue. Greater resources should be given to select committees to enable them to effectively monitor the work of quangos.

Major strategic documents that are intended to set the priorities of the organisation should be approved by select committees with an appropriate accountability measure requiring public bodies to report back to the select committee on delivery and, in particular, expenditure.

Departmental select committees are ideally placed to conduct greater scrutiny, and in the case of the House of Commons, have a minimum of 11 MPs, deciding upon the line of inquiry and then gather written and oral evidence.

It is not unreasonable to expect the Commons to work with the Lords' scrutiny system since Lords Select Committees typically do not shadow the work of government departments and their investigations look into specialist subjects, taking advantage of the Lords' expertise and the greater amount of time (compared to MPs) available to them to examine issues. Where matters are raised by the Commons, they could be passed to the Lords for in-depth scrutiny of the board of public bodies, memberships of committees or perceived errors in strategy.

It would also be helpful for Select Committees to be able to appeal to a deeper 'Scrutiny Reserve Resolution' on all work covering ALBs, since those bodies' independence are greater and far removed from parliament and so their scrutiny must be deepened. For example, in the European Union Committee of the House of Lords, the committee's scrutiny work has previously been underpinned by a 'Scrutiny Reserve Resolution', meaning that the Government has undertaken not to agree to any EU proposal until the Committee has completed its consideration, or cleared it from scrutiny. The same 'Scrutiny Reserve Resolution' applied to public bodies would mean the Government would undertake not to agree to any high-level public body proposal until the Select Committee had completed some consideration of the proposal, or cleared it from scrutiny. The overlap between the bodies of EU and our public bodies is a clear one: both suffer a democratic deficit in their legitimacy and ability to operate away from government itself, parliament and the public, and both have a scrutiny failing that must be remedied in a similar manner.

There are further things that can be done, that are more specific. Tim Ambler of the Adam Smith Institute has suggested there are unique changes at the departmental level that would improve the structure and relationship between government proper and public bodies:

- The **Department for Environment, Food and Rural Affairs** could: (i) pursue the 'Dutch model' and achieve a near-90 per cent reduction in headcount by delegating much of its role to local government; (ii) all NDPBs should be reclassified either as Executive Agencies (if they are operational arms of Defra) or as committees within the core (if they are simply advisory); (iii) there are total potential staff savings from its ALBs of 11,385, while the core department savings amount to 4,364, making 15,749 in total, approximately half the current headcount.[190]

- When reforming the **Department of Health and Social Care**: (i) it is unnecessary, for example, to have two ALBs duplicating each other in reviewing and licensing medicines and other health aids, so we should seek to retain the one with the wider remit (MHRA) and close NICE; (ii) All advisory bodies should be abolished, rather government might seek advice from experts as and when it is needed; and (iii) proposals have already suggested staff savings amount to 9,333 from ALBs and 2,330 from the core, a total of 11,663.[191]

- The **Department for Work and Pensions** could be better (i) restructured in line with the original Ibbs guidelines, namely a minimalist policy core with policies being delivered by executive agencies; while (ii) the 4,036 existing staff in its ALBs should be reduced to 3,108, with a probable saving of 928.[192]

- The **Department for Levelling Up, Housing & Communities** should look to review its core department needing (i) no more than 500 civil servants whose role should be limited to disbursing the funding and then evaluating the funded schemes to disseminate the more successful to other regions and local authorities while (ii) potential staff savings arising from reforms amount to 5,030 (88 per cent) saving out of 5,696 staff.[193]

- The **Department for Business, Energy and Industrial Strategy** could be reformed so that (i) all advisory ALBs should cease existence as formal bodies, and in which advisors can instead be called on as and when necessary; while (ii) all other ALBs should either become agencies or privatised if they are substantial, or merged into core or other bodies if they are not.[194]

Attempts have been made to reduce the number of 'quangos' – often referred to as a 'bonfire of the quangos' – and some progress has been made. It remains a concern that no single register exists, or a clear understanding of exactly how many quangos there are in full. Transparency would help us to debate the size of the bureaucratic state as well as the money spent on it. There will be many who simply think we should abolish large parts of government and those who would like to expand departments by bringing more of these ALBs into these departments – making them much less 'arm's length' but directly accountable to ministers. Reforming the quango state will sit somewhere in the middle, with a greater capacity for parliament to reduce expenditure and scrutinise the leadership and performance of these bodies, bringing them under democratic control.

Notes

1 https://www.gov.uk/government/statistics/public-spending-statistics-release-may-2022/public-spending-statistics-may-2022; Total government expenditure for 2020/21 was £566.2 billion in 'Departmental Expenditure Limits' and £489.8 billion in 'Annually Managed Expenditure'.
2 https://assets.publishing.service.gov.uk/government/uploads/system/uploads/attachment_data/file/690946/Public_Bodies_-_a_guide_for_departments_-_chapter_2.pdf
3 *Ibid.*
4 *Ibid.*
5 https://www.gov.uk/guidance/public-bodies-reform
6 https://assets.publishing.service.gov.uk/government/uploads/system/uploads/attachment_data/file/690636/Executive_Agencies_Guidance.PDF
7 Personal communication.
8 https://www.gov.uk/government/publications/public-bodies-review-programme/requirements-for-reviews-of-public-bodies#accountability
9 https://www.instituteforgovernment.org.uk/publication/whitehall-monitor-2022/arms-length-bodies
10 https://www.instituteforgovernment.org.uk/publication/whitehall-monitor-2022/arms-length-bodies
11 https://www.gov.uk/government/publications/public-bodies-2020
12 *Ibid.*
13 https://commonslibrary.parliament.uk/research-briefings/cbp-9148/
14 2016: https://publications.parliament.uk/pa/cm201617/cmselect/cmpubacc/488/488.pdf;
   2021: https://committees.parliament.uk/publications/7431/documents/77735/default/
15 https://www.instituteforgovernment.org.uk/publication/whitehall-monitor-2022/arms-length-bodies

16 https://policyexchange.org.uk/publication/bittersweet-success-glass-ceilings-for-britains-ethnic-minorities-at-the-top-of-business-and-the-professions/

17 https://allinbritain.org/gareth-southgate-and-identity-politics/

18 https://committees.parliament.uk/publications/8226/documents/84184/default/

19 https://www.instituteforgovernment.org.uk/publications/reforming-public-appointments

20 *Ibid.*

21 https://www.instituteforgovernment.org.uk/publication/whitehall-monitor-2022/arms-length-bodies

22 https://www.bbc.co.uk/news/uk-politics-57280438

23 https://www.independent.co.uk/news/uk/politics/boris-johnson-paul-dacre-ofcom-charles-moore-bbc-b627465.html

24 https://bbcgossip.com/news/former-daily-mail-editor-paul-dacre-blasts-liberal-civil-servants-as-he-quits-ofcom-chairman-race/

25 https://www.theguardian.com/education/2021/feb/10/former-tory-mp-in-row-over-appointment-as-head-of-office-for-students

26 https://www.theguardian.com/media/2018/jan/09/toby-young-resigns-office-for-students

27 https://www.theguardian.com/society/2021/dec/20/calls-for-re-run-of-selection-process-to-find-next-head-of-charity-commission

28 https://www.instituteforgovernment.org.uk/publication/whitehall-monitor-2022/arms-length-bodies

29 https://www.theguardian.com/society/2018/feb/21/mps-refuse-to-endorse-former-tory-minister-as-head-of-charity-commission

30 https://committees.parliament.uk/writtenevidence/37396/pdf/

31 Loughlin, M. (2010) *Foundations of Public Law.*

32 https://www.ons.gov.uk/methodology/classificationsandstandards/economicstatisticsclassifications/introductiontoeconomicstatisticsclassifications

33 https://www.gov.uk/government/organisations

34 https://www.nao.org.uk/wp-content/uploads/2021/06/Central-oversight-of-Arms-length-bodies-Summary.pdf

35 https://www.nao.org.uk/wp-content/uploads/2021/06/Central-oversight-of-Arms-length-bodies-Summary.pdf

36 https://www.nao.org.uk/wp-content/uploads/2021/06/Central-oversight-of-Arms-length-bodies.pdf

37 https://www.gov.uk/government/publications/quango-reform-public-bodies-closed-so-far

38 https://www.gov.uk/government/publications/how-to-appeal-to-the-civil-service-appeal-board/how-to-appeal-to-the-civil-service-appeal-board

39 https://aerc.org.uk/

40 https://assets.publishing.service.gov.uk/government/uploads/system/uploads/attachment_data/file/1001885/Public_Bodies_2020.pdf

41 https://www.nao.org.uk/wp-content/uploads/2016/05/Departments-oversight-of-arms-length-bodies-a-comparative-study.pdf

42 https://www.gov.uk/government/collections/impact-assessments-guidance-for-government-departments

43 https://www.nao.org.uk/wp-content/uploads/2016/05/Departments-oversight-of-arms-length-bodies-a-comparative-study.pdf

44 Sample restricted solely to organisations with a specific regulatory function.

45 https://assets.publishing.service.gov.uk/government/uploads/system/uploads/attachment_data/file/1028251/Updated_framework_document_v.final2.pdf

46 https://nic.org.uk/app/uploads/NIC-register-of-interests-2022-23.pdf

47 https://www.gov.uk/government/publications/the-low-pay-commissioners-register-of-interests-2022

48 https://www.whatdotheyknow.com/request/questions_about_transparency_mea_12#incoming-2121626

49 https://www.gov.uk/government/organisations/scientific-advisory-group-for-emergencies/about

50 https://assets.publishing.service.gov.uk/government/uploads/system/uploads/attachment_data/file/80087/sage-guidance.pdf

51 https://www.gov.uk/government/publications/scientific-advisory-group-for-emergencies-sage-coronavirus-covid-19-response-membership/list-of-participants-of-sage-and-related-sub-groups

52 https://www.bbc.co.uk/news/uk-politics-52553229

53 https://www.dailymail.co.uk/news/article-9076215/Did-No10-lie-Professor-Lockdown-quitting-SAGE.html

54 https://gbdeclaration.org/

55 Adam Smith, The Wealth of Nations, Penguin Books 2003.

56 https://data.spectator.co.uk/category/sage-scenarios

57 https://www.dailymail.co.uk/news/article-9076215/Did-No10-lie-Professor-Lockdown-quitting-SAGE.html

58 https://dailysceptic.org/archive/the-imperial-model-and-its-role-in-the-uks-pandemic-response/

59 Ibid.

60 https://www.spectator.co.uk/article/the-lockdown-files-rishi-sunak-on-what-we-werent-told

61 *Ibid.*

62 https://www.reuters.com/world/uk/uks-liz-truss-will-probe-extent-bank-england-independence-supporter-says-2022-08-04/

63 https://www.bankofengland.co.uk/about

64 https://www.ons.gov.uk/economy/inflationandpriceindices/timeseries/d7bt/mm23

65 https://www.independent.co.uk/news/business/at-last-independence-for-the-bank-1260188.html

66 https://www.theguardian.com/politics/1997/may/07/economy.uk

67 https://hansard.parliament.uk/Commons/1997-06-11/debates/ cc73185e-9f48-40b7-8907-87cefba8e8da/BankOfEngland?highlight=forced%20through%20many%20painful%20decisions%20bring%20down%20inflation%20they%20always%20acted%20late%20they%20rather%20their%20predecessors%20should%20have%20acted%20advance%20inflation%20appearing%20that%20what%20technically-based%20independent%20central%20bank#contribution-e680943d-428f-4422-b489-da0554e618cf

68 *Ibid.*

69 https://www.independent.co.uk/news/business/recession-interest-rates-inflation-bank-of-england-b2139012.html

70 https://www.bankofengland.co.uk/monetary-policy-report/2022/august-2022

71 https://www.bbc.co.uk/news/business-58098118

72 https://www.standard.co.uk/comment/bank-of-england-errors-inflation-andrew-bailey-uk-economy-b1038059.html

73 https://thecritic.co.uk/issues/november-2021/too-much-of-a-good-thing/

74 https://www.bankofengland.co.uk/boeapps/database/fromshowcolumns.asp?Travel=NIxSUx&FromSeries=1&ToSeries=50&DAT=RNG&FD=1&FM=Jan&FY=2010&TD=2&TM=Nov&TY=2022&FNY=&CSVF=TT&html.x=125&html.y=19&C=MEB&Filter=N; https://www.ons.gov.uk/economy/inflationandpriceindices/timeseries/d7bt/mm23; https://www.bankofengland.co.uk/monetary-policy/the-interest-rate-bank-rate

75 https://www.msn.com/en-us/money/markets/central-banks-e2-80-99-covid-qe-splurge-was-a-e2-80-98mistake-e2-80-99-ex-boe-governor-king-says/ar-AA13i0aG

76 *The Times,* Monday August 8 2022.
77 https://www.bankofengland.co.uk/monetary-policy/quantitative-easing
78 *Ibid.*
79 https://www.bankofengland.co.uk/climate-change
80 https://www.bankofengland.co.uk/-/media/boe/files/about/bank-of-england-out-and-proud-charter.pdf?la=en&hash=878616BD7DA47E7145F19DB3972E7633890688E6
81 https://www.express.co.uk/news/uk/1591828/Bank-of-England-logo-Britannia-woke-dyslexia-ont
82 https://www.bankofengland.co.uk/freedom-of-information/2021/boes-membership-with-stonewall-during-2019-2021
83 https://www.bankofengland.co.uk/speech/2019/mark-carney-investing-in-ethnicity-and-race-conference-2019-held-the-bank-of-england
84 https://www.msn.com/en-gb/money/other/ex-mandarin-with-e2-80-98no-economic-experience-e2-80-99-lined-up-for-bank-of-england-role/ar-AA10nAEc?fromMaestro=true
85 https://conservativehome.com/2022/11/28/john-redwood-being-in-office-does-not-mean-being-in-power/
86 https://www.telegraph.co.uk/politics/2023/02/04/liz-truss-downing-street-reflection-mini-budget-boris-johnson/
87 https://www.thetimes.co.uk/article/liz-truss-got-a-lot-wrong-but-is-right-that-ldis-amplified-market-turmoil-578mv80pw
88   https://www.telegraph.co.uk/business/2022/09/29/bank-england-warned-pension-funds-crisis-five-years-ago-next/
89 https://capx.co/did-liz-truss-really-cause-the-bond-market-rout/
90 *Ibid.*
91 https://www.thetimes.co.uk/article/rotherham-shows-policing-the-police-is-failing-badly-rnz2207zk
92 https://www.london-fire.gov.uk/about-us/independent-culture-review/
93 https://www.whatdotheyknow.com/request/807554/response/1931874/attach/html/2/FINAL%20RESPONSE%205023147%20Dave%20Bratt.pdf.html
94 https://uk.linkedin.com/in/sal-naseem-1aa5a829
95 https://www.policeconduct.gov.uk/sites/default/files/Documents/Who-we-are/our-people/ROI_27012023.pdf
96 https://www.report-it.org.uk/information_sharing_agreements
97 https://www.theyworkforyou.com/wrans/?id=2022-05-17.3745.h&s=tell+mama#g3745.r0

98 https://www.gov.uk/government/publications/police-super-complaints-designated-bodies/designated-bodies

99 https://www.whatdotheyknow.com/request/information_about_your_dealings_31#incoming-1758629

100 https://www.whatdotheyknow.com/request/862400/response/2061525/attach/html/2/5023558%20R%20Norrie%20response%20letter.pdf.html

101 https://www.whatdotheyknow.com/request/862400/response/2061525/attach/html/2/5023558%20R%20Norrie%20response%20letter.pdf.html

102 https://yougov.co.uk/topics/politics/articles-reports/2020/07/16/where-does-british-public-stand-transgender-rights

103 https://www.whatdotheyknow.com/request/862400/response/2061525/attach/html/2/5023558%20R%20Norrie%20response%20letter.pdf.html

104 https://www.whatdotheyknow.com/request/lgbt_matters_2

105 https://www.british-business-bank.co.uk/

106 https://www.british-business-bank.co.uk/corporate-information/

107 https://www.british-business-bank.co.uk/corporate-information/

108 https://en.wikipedia.org/wiki/British_Business_Bank

109 https://www.british-business-bank.co.uk/what-the-british-business-bank-does/

110 https://www.nao.org.uk/reports/british-business-bank/

111 *Ibid.*

112 https://www.bankofengland.co.uk/boeapps/database/fromshowcolumns.asp?Travel=NIxSTxTAxSUx&FromSeries=1&ToSeries=50&DAT= RNG&FD=1&FM=Jan&FY=2000&TD=20&TM=Jul&TY=2022&FNY=&CSVF=TT&html.x=86&html.y=33&C=OCZ&C=OCB&C=UKC&C=UK6&Filter=N

113 https://www.dailymail.co.uk/news/article-10761159/Russian-crime-syndicates-able-ransack-UK-public-purse-Covid-loans-MP-says.html

114 https://www.bbc.co.uk/news/business-59504943

115 https://www.bbc.co.uk/news/business-59504943

116 https://www.bbc.co.uk/news/av/uk-55895738

117 https://www.nao.org.uk/report/the-bounce-back-loan-scheme-an-update/

118 https://www.theyworkforyou.com/wrans/?id=2022-03-25.147033.h

119 https://www.bbc.co.uk/news/business-59504943

120 https://www.bbc.co.uk/news/business-59504943

121 https://www.bbc.co.uk/news/uk-politics-60117513

122 https://hansard.parliament.uk/Lords/2022-01-24/debates/805E6270-7DF6-4CF8-9487-08F9028A1EE1/CoronavirusGrantSchemesFraud#contribution-938D95C8-A537-4056-9523-F6156A854EF5

123 *Ibid.*

124 https://www.dailymail.co.uk/news/article-11024455/Rishi-Sunak-accused-peddling-fairytale-Covid-loans-scheme-ex-minister-Lord-Agnew.html

125 https://www.whatdotheyknow.com/request/bounce_back_loan_scheme_fraud_cl#incoming-2010496

126 https://www.whatdotheyknow.com/request/784189/response/1873134/attach/html/3/FOI%2021%20096%20Final%20Response.pdf.html

127 https://www.nao.org.uk/wp-content/uploads/2021/07/Investigation-into-the-British-Business-Banks-accreditation-of-Greensill-Capital.pdf

128 https://www.british-business-bank.co.uk/press-release/recovery-loan-scheme-offers-over-4-5bn-of-lending-to-smaller-businesses/

129 https://hansard.parliament.uk/Lords/2014-07-08/debates/140708114000210/IndustrialStrategyBritishBusinessBank

130 https://www.british-business-bank.co.uk/annual-report-and-accounts-2021/

131 https://www.nao.org.uk/reports/british-business-bank/

132 https://www.british-business-bank.co.uk/investing-in-women-code/code/

133 https://www.british-business-bank.co.uk/press-release/british-business-bank-commissioned-to-convene-a-working-group-on-access-to-capital-for-entrepreneurs-to-feed-into-the-prime-ministers-commission-on-race-and-ethnic-disparities/

134 https://www.theguardian.com/world/2021/apr/03/business-chiefs-say-their-advice-ignored-in-no-10s-race-report

135 https://www.ethnicity-facts-figures.service.gov.uk/workforce-and-business/business/access-to-start-up-loans/latest

136 https://thecritic.co.uk/stirring-the-melting-pot/

137 https://www.telegraph.co.uk/technology/2020/07/18/secretive-uk-fund-behind-governments-500m-investment-oneweb/

138 https://www.nao.org.uk/wp-content/uploads/2020/01/British-Business-Bank.pdf

139 *Ibid.*

140 https://en.wikipedia.org/wiki/British_Business_Bank

141 https://www.dailymail.co.uk/news/article-11105241/Frustrated-Brits-demand-action-water-firms-fix-leaks-hosepipe-ban-drought-UK.html

142 https://www.bbc.co.uk/news/business-62464387

143 https://www.bbc.co.uk/news/science-environment-56590219

144 https://www.dailymail.co.uk/news/article-10503873/Fury-water-companies-make-2-8BILLION-profits-amid-scandal-dumping-raw-sewage-rivers.html

145 https://www.bbc.co.uk/news/business-62464387

146 https://www.OFWAT.gov.uk/OFWAT-reveals-progress-on-water-industry-leakage-performance/

147 https://anglingtrust.net/2022/08/16/OFWAT-20-years-of-regulatory-failure/

148 *Ibid.*

149 https://www.msn.com/en-gb/money/other/OFWAT-boss-accused-of-not-getting-tough-on-leak-targets/ar-AA10JvKC

150 https://www.theguardian.com/environment/2022/aug/16/OFWAT-chief-defends-water-companies-over-lack-of-new-reservoirs

151 https://anglingtrust.net/2022/08/16/OFWAT-20-years-of-regulatory-failure/

152 https://www.OFWAT.gov.uk/about-us/equality-diversity-and-inclusion-edi/

153 FOI request.

154 https://heycar.co.uk/guides/dvla-medical-licence-guide

155 https://www.whatdotheyknow.com/request/staff_numbers_and_live_applicati
DVLA statisticians were unable to separate out paper correspondence from paper applications, but it assumed the two correlate, giving a reliable denominator to measure the level of demand placed upon it.

156 *Ibid,* https://www.nao.org.uk/wp-content/uploads/2022/11/backlogs-in-driving-licence-applications.pdf

157 https://www.nao.org.uk/wp-content/uploads/2022/11/backlogs-in-driving-licence-applications.pdf

158 https://www.nao.org.uk/wp-content/uploads/2022/11/backlogs-in-driving-licence-applications.pdf

159 https://www.bbc.co.uk/news/57810729

160 https://assets.publishing.service.gov.uk/government/uploads/system/uploads/attachment_data/file/1090804/DVLA_annual_report_and_accounts_2021_to_2022.pdf

161 https://www.sportengland.org/about-us#whoweare-12165
162 https://www.maslaha.org/Project/Muslim-Girls-Fence-
163 https://www.maslaha.org/
164 https://www.youtube.com/watch?v=Pegea8eWOW0
165 https://www.sportengland.org/about-us#whoweare-12165
166 https://www.migrantsorganise.org/our-campaigns/patients-not-passports/
167 https://www.migrantsorganise.org/why-is-rwanda-plan-wrong-and-what-can-we-do-about-it/
168 https://www.voice4change-england.org/post/rwanda-deportation-racist-narratives-about-asylum-seeker-and-refugee
169 https://www.sportengland.org/about-us#whoweare-12165
170 https://www.voice4change-england.org/about-4
171 https://find-and-update.company-information.service.gov.uk/company/02719699/filing-history
172 https://www.thetimes.co.uk/article/at-a-certain-point-pumping-in-money-doesnt-help-and-i-think-were-there-2dfxhzws0
173 https://www.legislation.gov.uk/ukpga/2008/27/part/2
174 https://www.gov.uk/guidance/carbon-budgets
175 Based on 255 working days in a year.
176 https://www.gov.uk/government/publications/public-bodies-2020
177 Ibid.
178 https://www.telegraph.co.uk/news/2021/12/04/climate-change-committee-has-vastly-overplayed-hand/
179 https://www.theccc.org.uk/publication/2022-progress-report-to-parliament/
180 https://www.independent.co.uk/climate-change/news/cop26-uk-climate-lord-deben-b1948028.html
181 https://www.theccc.org.uk/publication/ucl-sustainable-health-equity-achieving-a-net-zero-uk/
182 https://www.theccc.org.uk/2020/11/06/ccc-welcomes-independent-report-on-climate-change-and-health/
183 https://www.theccc.org.uk/wp-content/uploads/2022/11/CCC-Gifts-and-Hospitality-Register_Nov-22.xlsx
184 https://iea.org.uk/publications/hot-air-a-critique-of-the-uks-climate-change-committee/
185 https://www.ceres.tech/
186 Thomas Sowell, (1987) A Conflict of Visions.
187 https://www.gov.uk/government/organisations/social-mobility-commission

188 https://www.politicshome.com/thehouse/article/to-ensure-the-pms-words-have-a-bite-the-social-mobility-commission-must-have-real-teeth

189 *Ibid.*

190 https://static1.squarespace.com/static/56eddde762cd9413e151ac92/t/635004c8165c120dbbdf821f/1666188489059/Food+for+Thought+Version+1.pdf

191 *Ibid.*

192 *Ibid.*

193 *Ibid.*

194 *Ibid.*

CIVITAS

Subscriptions and Membership (UK only)
If you would like to stay abreast of Civitas' latest work, you can have all of our books delivered to your door as soon as they are published. New subscribers receive a free copy of Roger Bootle's book, *The AI Economy: Work, Wealth and Welfare in the Robot Age* and Daniel Bentley's book, *The Land Question* on fixing the dysfunction at the root of the housing crisis. For those who would like to support our work further and get involved in our Westminster events, we have a variety of Subscription and Membership options available:
https://www.civitasonline.org.uk/product-category/subscriptions/

We regret that we are unable to post items to non-UK residents, although all of our publications are individually available via our Civitas Book Store (https://www.civitasonline.org.uk) and in most cases on Amazon.

Renewals for Existing Members

If you are an existing member wishing to renew with ease and convenience, please do select one of the subscription or membership options that most closely meets your requirements.

Make a Donation

If you like our work and would like to help see it continue, please consider making a donation. A contribution of any amount, big or small, will help us advance our research and educational activities. You can make a donation by getting in touch (020 7799 6677) or sending a simple email to info@civitas.org.uk so that we can come back to you.

Supporters of Civitas

Because we want to reach as wide an audience as possible, our subscription and membership fees are set as low as possible and barely meet printing and postage expenses. To meet the costs of producing our research and conducting our educational projects, we rely entirely on the goodwill and generosity of people who value our work.

If you would like to support our work on a rolling basis, there is a variety of advanced membership levels on offer. Supporters of Civitas have the opportunity to become more deeply engaged with the work their philanthropy makes possible.

You can pay by selecting a membership or subscription option and we will be in contact.

Alternatively, just call us on +44 (0)20 7799 6677
or email info@civitas.org.uk and we can discuss your options.

If it is your preference, please make cheques payable to Civitas.

Civitas: Institute for the Study of Civil Society
First Floor
55 Tufton Street
Westminster
London
SW1P 3QL

Email: subs@civitas.org.uk